ENDORSEMENTS

Attributing all to God's glory, Alton tells of fifty years of ministry in Brazil. It is a story of hard work, perseverance, faith, sacrifice, love for the Lord and His people, and outreach to those who do not know Him. For a time, we had the privilege of being co-workers with Alton and Ebba. Their lives and their story are genuine, loving, faithful and challenging.

—*Earl Whittaker*
Veteran Missionary and Pastor

Alton Cothron and I were in youth group together at our church in Colorado. His parents drove Alton and others of us to California to begin our training as missionaries. There's never been any doubt in my mind about Alton's dedication to the Lord—his humor, his listening ear, his quick intelligence, his humility all played a part in making Jesus known wherever he might be. Because I served in a different country, I knew very little about his and Ebba's work in Brazil. Time after time while editing his book, I saw trials that would have cause many to give up—but not Alton! To quote Julie Andrews, "Steadiness is coming up short 19 times and succeeding on the twentieth."

—*Maxine Morarie*
Veteran Missionary to Bolivia, and Editor

Alton Cothron thinks, lives, and breathes missions. Having been called to the mission field at fourteen, Alton embarked on a life-long ministry in Brazil at twenty-two. With his wife, Ebba, at his side, Alton evangelized and discipled, while church planting, training, and overseeing for over fifty years. With a passion to see the unevangelized reached, Alton challenges and encourages through regular letters and email many who have been impacted by his ministry. Amazingly, at 95 years of age, Alton continues to teach two Bible studies weekly. To God be the glory!

—Daniel Steinman
Pastor, Freedom Baptist Church of Chesapeake, VA

This book tells a remarkable story: the story of Alton and Ebba Cothron, an American missionary couple who dedicated their lives to Brazil so that the unreached could hear the good news of Jesus Christ. I deeply appreciate their love for Jesus, for Brazil, and for Brazilians. I met Alton and Ebba in Brazil and was trained by both of them. I am delighted that their life story is now documented and published. I highly recommend this book as an inspiring example of how our love for Jesus can be transformed into a love for people among the nations.

Jairo de Oliveira holds a PhD in Intercultural Studies and is an adjunct professor at Columbia International University (CIU). He is based in the Middle East with his family, where he works with refugees.

—Jairo

THIS FASCINATING
THING CALLED
Missions

ALTON G. COTHRON

THIS FASCINATING THING CALLED
Missions

EQUIP PRESS

Colorado Springs

THIS FASCINATING THING CALLED Missions

Published by Equip Press, Colorado Springs, CO

First Edition: 2024
This Facinating Thing Called Missions / Alton G. Cothron
Paperback ISBN: 978-1-958585-78-8
eBook ISBN: 978-1-958585-90-0

EQUIP PRESS

Colorado Springs

IN APPRECIATION

I am sincerely grateful, first, for an Almighty, Faithful God who prompted me to write this book, and for Ebba, whose name brought smiles to my eyes whenever I included her in the text; and for the friends and colleagues who encouraged me and made suggestions. I am especially indebted to my dear life-long friend, Maxine Morarie, for her willingness to edit our story.

This book is dedicated to all the young people
who sense God tugging at their hearts as they read our story.
*Give Him your life and you will be amazed
at what he will do with it!*

BACKGROUND

For a few years, I considered writing a history of the ministry that my wife, Ebba, and I had in Brazil, South America. Originally, the plan was to leave something behind for our children and grandchildren. But as the idea began to take hold we received encouragement from mission colleagues and friends here in the States to make the project a little larger than I first intended, and to publish our memoirs in book-form, making it available to a larger audience. This seemed justified, since so many people, members, and friends of New Tribes Mission have had a part in our ministry through prayer, encouragement, and financial support during the fifty wonderful years Ebba and I spent in Brazil. It is impossible to mention each of you by name, but we praise the Lord for all of you and thank you for the part you have had in all that the Lord was able to accomplish through our service.

Ethnos360 is now the official name of the mission, but because New Tribes Mission was the term used during our years of service in Brazil, that is the term that will generally be used in the text of this book, which focuses on our lives and the places we lived and worked. This book is not intended to be a complete history of New Tribes Mission's activities in Brazil during the years we spent there. It does, however, include people and places pertinent to our story. In writing the events it might seem we put ourselves first and others in a secondary light, but that was not our intention. We gladly and humbly give God all the glory and praise for everything of eternal value that has been done through us, simple clay vessels that we are. It is our sincere desire that all who read this history will find encouragement and be challenged to let God use *your life* in some way, somewhere, for the salvation of souls and the advancement of the Kingdom of God.

Since Ebba and I didn't just drop out of the sky into Brazil, a brief biography of our lives prior to becoming involved in missionary work is not only justified, but necessary: what took place during the approximate twenty years before we became members of New Tribes Mission and ended up in Brazil?

Our paths began separately, Ebba's on April 9, 1931 in Muskegon Heights, Michigan; mine on January 24, 1929, in Denver, Colorado. Our paths *really* joined in July of 1952 when we married. Our childhood years, teenage years, schooling, and upbringing were quite normal for Americans in the 1930's and 1940's.

Ebba came from a family of five children: four girls and one boy. Her father, George R. Olson, was born of Swedish parents and lived in a Swedish community until seventeen years of age. After graduating from business college, George took a job at a large foundry in Muskegon Heights, Michigan, where he moved gradually into a managerial position. He retired after over forty years with this company. Unfortunately, he did not enjoy retirement for very long, for a few months later, at age sixty-five, he died of a heart attack.

Mayme Haines Olson, Ebba's mother, was of English descent, and a schoolteacher. Velma, Ebba's older sister, was instrumental in leading her mother to Christ, and soon after, her father was also saved. The family became active members of Oakwood Baptist Church near their home on Fifth Street in Muskegon Heights.

Ebba played the clarinet in her high school band. A highlight for her was when her school's band was given the opportunity to practice and perform with the University of Michigan Band. When she graduated from high school in 1949, she also had completed two years of Bible school, which she had attended evenings in Grand Rapids since 1947. It was during this time that missionaries from New Tribes Mission (NTM) came to Oakwood Baptist Church. They were invited to the Olson's home, and through them, Ebba felt the call to be a missionary. Her parents always opened their home to missionaries, and they encouraged Ebba to obey her call. In July of 1949, one couple and three single girls from their church, Ebba among them, took off for California to enroll in the NTM Training Center. All three girls from Oakwood Baptist have spent their lives in missionary work.

My parents first met at Judson Baptist Church in south Denver where my mother, Marguerite Z. Cohenour, sang in the choir. Granville Cothron, my father, was born in 1896 in Lafayette, Tennessee, and was saved at an early age. He arrived in Denver in the late 1920's from Texas. Mother was born in Fairbury, Nebraska in 1894, and was also saved at an early age. She moved to Denver before the turn of the century.

My father soon decided that farming on the steep, rocky hillsides where he was raised was not what he wanted in life, so at the first opportunity he joined the army, where he served for seven years. At least two of those years were spent in France and Germany, where he saw heavy combat service during the First World War. At another period of military service my father was part of the American forces that pursued the bandit Poncho Villa around northern Mexico. It was after his military service that my father finally came to Denver, married, raised a family, worked, and died in 1987 at age ninety-one.

My mother took business school in Denver and studied voice and piano. She was a good musician. As a child, I remember her students coming to our house for voice lessons. Mom and Dad were always faithful in church and taught Sunday School classes, did visitation, and sang in the choir. My sister, Lyda, and I were blessed to have received good biblical teaching at home and in church from the time we were born, and we both became missionaries.

I attended Lowell Grade School, Englewood Junior & Senior High School, and graduated in 1947. Since I planned to become a medical doctor, I entered the University of Denver that fall to prepare for a career in medicine. However, prior to this at the age of fourteen, I had been challenged to missions by two different missionaries, one from China and one from Africa. I knew that this was still what God wanted for my life. The struggle was finally over when I let God have his way. The straw that broke the camel's back, to use an old saying, was when Mr. Les Pedersen from New Tribes Mission visited First Christian Church (later called Englewood Bible Church) and challenged the young people to consider giving their lives to reach tribes still unreached and forgotten. Several of us responded to the challenge and after training with the mission in California, many of us ended up on the mission field in South America. This is where the story of the Alton and Ebba Cothron's missionary career begins!

CONTENTS

CHAPTER ONE

TRIBAL MISSIONARY TRAINING

A member of New Tribes Mission (NTM) spoke at our church and told us about tribal people throughout the world whose languages had never been written, who were still illiterate, who had never heard of the Bible or of God's plan of salvation. He showed us a film of five men preparing to enter the Bolivian jungle to look for a tribe resistant to civilization and noted for its raids and killings; the film ended with five smiling men, waving goodbye to their co-workers who were filming them. After the film, the NTM speaker told us the scenes we had seen were filmed six years before in 1943, and gave us the shocking news that the five men were never seen again, and were presumed to be dead. He left us with this challenge: "Would you be willing to give your life to reach the forgotten people of the world with the Gospel?" I was one of five singles who responded in the affirmative to this challenge.

In the fall of 1949, two couples and five single folks from my church in Englewood, Colorado headed for Fouts Springs, California, where NTM had established its training program for missionary candidates.

The day we drove into Fouts Springs, I saw Ebba Olson for the first time and something inside me said, *that is the girl you will marry.* She was working along with other students, helping to put a roof on one of the new cabins being built to accommodate the large group of new candidates that would be arriving.

Fouts Springs had been a CCC Camp (Civilian Conservation Corps) where unemployed, unskilled young men could earn their board and keep by working on projects for the government during the depression years; some of the original buildings were still there when NTM moved in, but these were not in the best of condition, nor adequate to handle the increase of new missionary candidates. One of the first things we noticed when we arrived was all the building going on: cabins, dormitories, and auditorium.

The training school was located approximately fifty miles west of the town of Willows. Part of the road into camp was paved, but the unpaved portion was narrow, full of curves, winding its way over the mountains and down into the valley where the school was located. Some of the candidates, not used to such roads and fearful of driving on them, vowed they would not leave Fouts Springs until they had finished their training and were ready to go to the mission field!

Everyone referred to the training we received as *Boot Camp,* for that is what it resembled. Everything was geared to learning to live on the bare minimum of finances and rations to simulate what it could be like in other places of the world where we would one day be living. There was no electricity, running water, stores, and to say it was a little on the primitive side would be to do it justice: especially when we first arrived. We cooked and heated with wood burning stoves and carried water in pails from a spigot uphill from our cabins.

I was assigned to one of the last old CCC Camp buildings, which was being used as a dormitory for single men (because, I think, we would have a better chance of surviving if it collapsed upon us!) Our number of occupants varied from eight to fourteen men over the year that I was at Fouts Springs. There was no central dining hall for the students, as in most institutions. The members of each dormitory cooked for themselves. In ours, we took turns and cooked for a week at a time. This was good training, although not all meals were first-class. At one period we had a professional cook in our midst, and he helped those of us with less cooking experience.

One cooking incident merits telling, and that is how one of the fellows in our dorm came up with a very practical solution to his week as cook. Elmer decided to serve pancakes the entire week, and to make enough on the first day to last all week. We thought he was kidding, but sure enough, when we returned to the dorm after work detail, there were stacks of pancakes on the shelves in the kitchen. One of our members, by the name of Howard, said, "No way am I going to eat cold, hard pancakes the rest of the week!" And after supper, he threw most of them into the garbage. Some hot words flowed between Elmer and Howard, and it looked like they might come to blows. It all ended peaceably, however, and only Elmer ate the few pancakes he salvaged from the garbage for the rest of the week. (I can't remember what the rest of us ate!)

Two men in the dorm were well-liked and respected by all: Elmer Rabe (not the Elmer who made the pancakes) and Dave Yarwood. My bunk was next to Dave's. He had come to Boot Camp before I did, and I really looked up to him and his walk with the Lord. He went to Brazil before I did, and shortly after I arrived in Brazil in November of 1951, word was received that Dave had been killed by the tribe he had helped contact in western Brazil. The whole tribe abandoned the camp after the killing and the contact was lost. I was in Goiania when I learned that Dave had given his life, and remembered how closely he walked with the

Lord, and I knew that he'd received the "well-done, good and faithful servant" when he saw Jesus.

Elmer Rabe was a big man, very heavy, but also very strong, with lots of stamina. We were harvesting our firewood from a huge log outside the dorm that was close to three feet in diameter and perhaps fifteen feet long. We used a crosscut saw and each day we sawed off a slice and chopped it into pieces for the stove. It took two of us, taking turns, to cut through the log. But Elmer would grab the handle of the saw and before you knew it, he'd lift the slice he'd cut, and work it into stove links! He'd carry it inside, as though it had taken no effort at all. Whatever took strength to accomplish, Elmer would wear us all out trying to keep up with him.

Elmer married and went to Senegal, Africa with his family, where he worked faithfully for many years despite the hard things he faced there, one of which was the death of his son, who was snatched off the shore of the river by a crocodile. Elmer is now with the Lord also, and I'm sure he's praising God with all that wonderful strength of his.

Boot Camp was good training. We learned many things that prepared us for our service among tribal groups. Morning classes were: Bible, linguistics, how to plant a New Testament church in a tribal setting, field medicine, health, and culture. Afternoons were dedicated to a variety of maintenance and construction jobs. One of the everyday jobs was that of going up into the mountains with a truck to get firewood for the people in camp. It was hard work but enjoyable, too. Sometimes there were services in the evenings, and always on Sunday. We had some good hymn-sings, which included some of the songs composed by a couple of the men that had been killed by the Ayore in the early 40's, and by Paul Fleming, founder of NTM, who also shared his challenging messages with us when he would visit Boot Camp. Some of the students with cars would go out on weekends to visit churches in towns and cities in northern California.

I hadn't been in Boot Camp very long before meeting Jack Vaughn, another new student, and finding out that he enjoyed singing as much as I did. Jack played an autoharp which was our accompaniment, and we began singing duets, mostly missionary challenge songs. At the end of our year of training, we were privileged to travel with Macon Hare and Clayton Templeton as Representatives for New Tribes Mission. For three and a half months we traveled from coast to coast, from Chicago to Florida, and many points in between. Macon and Clayton did the preaching, while Jack and I furnished the music.

After the year's training was finished, candidates who joined New Tribes Mission, were set apart for ministry. We bid each other farewell and returned to our home churches and loved ones, preparing to go to the fields that God had laid on our hearts; some of these fields were in South America, others in the Far East.

The mission had purchased a small ship for the purpose of transporting missionaries to South America, and many of us booked passage on it. Both Ebba and I were aboard the MV Tribesman, as the ship was called, not as a couple, however. That would come later! We left October 15, 1951, from the west coast of the United States headed for Brazil.

CHAPTER TWO

ARRIVAL AND EVENTFUL BEGINNINGS

*T*he three-week journey from the west coast of the United States, through the Panama Canal and the Atlantic voyage southward, was almost over. We were finally arriving on the mission field, bonified members of New Tribes Mission!

On the way down, I said nothing to others on the ship about my biggest fear; perhaps I was too proud to admit what I felt. I look back now with a chuckle, but at the time it was serious business for me. Very simply stated: I was afraid I would not learn to speak Portuguese fluently! In my imagination, I could see others speaking with no difficulty, while I was struggling. Maybe this was because, in high school, studying foreign languages had no appeal to me. The *enemy* is clever and knows just what to throw at us to discourage us and make us want to turn back. But when he does this the Spirit of God raises up a standard against him! I was about to see how victorious God is over the devil, and how able he is to handle the unfounded fears the enemy puts in our hearts!

Our ship docked in Belem, and soon customs and immigration officials swarmed aboard. Much to my surprise, Captain Bagley, called me aside and said: "Alton, would you please take one of these officials on a tour of the ship?" I'm sure his request was based purely on showing courtesy and establishing good relationships with the Brazilian custom's personnel, but God had another thing in mind! He was going to use this contact with the immigration official to remove the fear I had about learning Portuguese.

The man I accompanied about the ship was very friendly, and took an interest in teaching me his language. He would point to different objects, such as trucks, trees, buildings, and what-have-you, pronounce them slowly and clearly, and invite me to say them. As I did so, I began to realize that I had no difficulty understanding what he said, and not only that, very little trouble in pronouncing the words. My fear vanished like an early morning fog when the sun shines on it. From that time on, I joyfully attacked, with vim and vigor, the task of learning the language that I would use for many, many years to come.

After going through immigration and customs (*alfandega*, in Portuguese) we collected our baggage, and were taken to a large, impressive, old house located in the outskirts of Belem. In anticipation of our arrival, Carl Taylor and Wayne Deason, missionaries with NTM in Brazil, had located this establishment for us, and were on hand when we arrived in Belem to escort us to it. What a relief to have a place to call home until we moved to more permanent locations in different parts of Brazil. The house may have been old, but the view was breathtaking: it overlooked the Amazon River!

The first night there, however, was unbelievable: not in a good sense, but challenging in every aspect! Everything was makeshift! Hammocks were strung up all over. Later, my wife Ebba, when sharing this story, said, "I had purchased a jungle hammock from a surplus store, but had never slept in one before. I had no idea the skill it took to keep right-side-up!"

There were five of us singles, two guys and three girls. Very gentlemanly, we fellows offered to hang the hammocks for the girls. Most of us had never hung a hammock before, much less slept in one, but *'how hard could it be,'* we thought. When the girls reclined in their hammocks, however, the ropes came untied, dumping them out on the floor! This made for a very short night: hanging and rehanging hammocks! Once gingerly in our hammocks, we dared not move a muscle for fear of undoing the ropes and finding ourselves on the floor again! (Sad to say, I never, in all the years to come, was comfortable in a hammock, though I had to sleep in them on many occasions!) The sleeping facilities for families were no better! Sheets were hung to partition one family's "territory" from another's: privacy was of no importance.

For some reason, on our first night, there was no electricity. Several of us hurried to a nearby store to buy candles and matches. What a riot! Of course, we didn't know the names of the items we wanted, so we resorted to gestures and perusing the shelves to locate them. Finally, with much patience on the part of the merchant, we headed back to our dark dwelling with candles (*velas*) and matches (*fosforos*). How many missionaries can say that the very first words they learned were *candles* and *matches?*

Prior to our arrival, someone had purchased a huge, clay water-filter. We were firmly instructed: '*Do not drink water which has not first been boiled and filtered!*' Gradually we acquired the food staples and other necessities, and life began to look a lot more possible for us newly arrived missionaries.

Growing in the backyard of our temporary home were several banana trees. Jack Vaughn and I decided to get ourselves some of the fruit. Who would go up the tree for the bananas? I was smaller than Jack, and perhaps more agile, more monkey-like. So, I grabbed a big knife, scaled the tree, and came down with a ripening stalk of bananas, quite satisfied with myself: until I learned I'd done it all wrong! Google it, and you can learn how harvesting bananas is supposed to be done!

During the first week in Brazil, we were taken to the Federal Police Department in downtown Belem to be properly documented, fingerprinted, and to receive our permanent ID, known as *'Modelo 19.'* Now that our papers were in order, we were free to travel. The decision was made where each would go. Five of us, the three single girls, and the two single fellows, would go south to the city of Goiania. Some of the families would travel up the Amazon River to Manaus, the capital of the state of Amazonas, situated in the heart of the Amazon Rainforest, 900 miles inland from the Atlantic coast. Others would remain in Belem, but the next thing we all faced, wherever our destination, was language study.

Sad to say, several who had come down on the ship, left within a few months, and returned to the United States. There were various reasons for this, but discouragement and culture shock were the main factors.

Early one morning, a few days after receiving our *Modelo 19s,* our mission pilots, Bill Post and Clem Smith, drove us five singles to the airport. We were weighed along with our baggage, and stepped into the big, single-engine Norseman, and took off for Goiania, the capital of the state of Goias, a thousand miles south of Belem.

In 1951, the only way to reach Goiania from Belem was by air - no highways for motor vehicles existed at that time. The trip took most of the day, with two stops for refueling, one in Carolina, in the state of Maranhão, and the other in a small town called Peixe, in the state of Goias. As we flew, we looked for villages of indigenous groups living in the jungles below, characteristic of the Timbira-Gavião, the Canela, the Krahô, and the Krinkati peoples. It was exciting when a village was spotted. From the air, the village looked like a big wagon wheel with houses around the rim, with paths like spokes, leading to the center, or *hub*, where, we learned later, meetings were held, and decisions and plans made by tribal leaders. Most of the land below us, however, was void of villages: just one huge carpet of forest.

Late in the afternoon, we landed in Goiania, and were taken to the homes of Carl Taylor and Clem Smith (one of our pilots). We received a warm welcome.

I was somewhat surprised as we circled to land, to see below us a city, rather than a village! Goiania, in November of 1951, was considered a relatively new city. It was less than thirty five years old, but had already reached a population of sixty thousand people. It was hard to believe that such a modern city existed in the interior of Brazil. Electric lights, running water, paved streets *and ice cream* were things I had not expected to find so far inland. In fact, before coming to Brazil, I tried to convince my mother that I did not need to take a dress suit and tie, because I would be in the jungle where formal attire would not be necessary! One look, though, at how modern Goiania was, made me glad my mother had won that battle.

NTM was still a new mission at the time, and was just opening works in several countries in South America. Brazil was one of those newly-forming fields, and we who had come, a boatload of us, were helping to beef up the much-needed personnel. With the arrival of five new missionaries, the NTM team in Goiania now numbered eleven people: team coordinator, Carl Taylor with his wife Cora; two pilots: Clem Smith with his wife Cecilia, and Bill Post with his wife Eloise; and five single missionaries: Jack Vaughn, Ebba Olson, Dee Bleigh, Myrtle Rehn, and Alton Cothron.

The first item of business was to find residences for the new arrivals. Jack and I would stay with Clem and Cecilia temporarily, and the three girls with the Taylors. The second item of business: finding ways for the new arrivals to learn Portuguese!

Carl Taylor lost no time finding a teacher for us. A converted Roman Catholic priest, by the name of Geraldo who knew some English, agreed to fill that position. By January of 1952, the girls had been placed in individual Brazilian homes where no English was spoken, and you might say, they were *forced* to use Portuguese. There is a more elegant term for this type of learning a language: *in-country immersion.* The great thing about immersion learning in-country is the acquisition of culture along with language.

Jack and I were "shipped out" to different interior towns for the same purpose. After Geraldo had given us a brief introduction to Portuguese, we began our own adventures into in-country immersion learning: discovering the colloquialisms of the language in this region, how the common people lived, and what they believed. You'll hear more about this as the story moves along.

During the seven weeks we were in Goiania (December 1951 to January 1952) there were important events taking place in the Brazilian branch of NTM, which would affect me and how God was to use me. But first, I'd like to share what took place to change my life forever, not too long after our arrival!

A little background is necessary to understand this life-changing event. You may remember something I wrote at the start of this history; if not, I will refresh your mind: the first time I saw Ebba Olson when I arrived in Fouts Springs for missionary training, I had a strong feeling that someday she would become my wife! We had never really dated except for a couple of times, but much prayer had gone into the matter.

So on the evening of December 15, 1951 I asked Ebba Olson if she would marry me. Ebba claims she never did say "Yes," but that I took her stunned silence as an affirmative answer! Well, whatever the case, she did not turn me down! We were married and served the Lord together for a few days short of 65 years, until the Lord called Ebba home in June of 2017. I've had no regrets that it was Ebba I chose to be my wife!

CHAPTER THREE

INTO THE INTERIOR WITH JOEL

S hortly after my proposal to Ebba, our team in Goiania had a meeting in the living room of Clem Smith's home, which was both devotional and business in nature. And that is where we broke the news of our engagement.

Wow, talk about surprises! Our team leader, Carl Taylor, couldn't believe what he was hearing and had the job of convincing us to set the wedding date ahead a few months, so that we could both adjust to the rigors of learning a new language, and gaining some experience in ministry, prior to taking on that of adjusting to marriage. It was decided that July 25, 1952, would be the date for our wedding, and we began laying plans!

When Abe Koop arrived in Goiania for the Field Conference, we'd hang out together and catch up on what had been happening in our lives since we'd last seen each other in Boot Camp. No doubt Abe and Dee Bleigh had sensed an attraction for each other during their Boot Camp training because it didn't take long after meeting up again in Goiania for them to announce their engagement! They were married near the end of 1952.

We five who came down to Brazil on the mission ship, and Abe who preceded us to Brazil, may have arrived single, but when furlough time came, we all returned to the States married! Jack Vaughn had left his fiancée in the United States, but she soon followed him to Brazil, and they were married in 1953. It took Myrtle Rehn a bit longer than the rest to meet her *prince charming*, Keith Wardlaw, but they eventually found each other and were married and worked for many years with the Yanomami in northern Brazil.

We were glad that we arrived in Brazil in time for its first Field Conference. It was held not far from the Taylor's home in the Evangelical Christian Church (*Igreja Crista Evangélica*) in Goiania. Due to the enormous distances, however, not all the NTM personnel were able to attend, but as I recall, there were 25-30 of us participating. At this point, we had not become an official entity with the Brazilian Government, but with the aid of a lawyer, Dr. Borba, a friend of Carl Taylor's, we became known officially as a mission a few years after that first Field Conference.

Following the conference, several of us went to Anápolis, a city about forty miles northeast, to visit some friends and a hospital. After a couple of days, Joel and I stayed behind in Anapolis when Ebba and the others returned to Goiania. And what happened next was what really began my ministry in Brazil.

While still in Goiania, Carl Taylor had introduced me to Joel Ferraz and said, "Alton, it's time you spread your wings and begin to fly! Joel has agreed to go interior with you as a companion and teacher. You'll leave Goiania and spend six months visiting small towns and evangelizing as you go."

Not having any idea of what was ahead, Joel and I took off, headed for Ceres. I was so glad Joel spoke English, and then he stuck a pin in my balloon! Right away he let me know how things stood. "Alton, I will only use English as a last resort, we're going to speak only Portuguese from now on. Agreed?"

We boarded a bus for the town of Ceres, almost 100 miles away. I was about to begin one of the most eventful times of my life! What a trip: miles and miles of unpaved roads, full of either mud or dust the entire way. It was hard to discern which was worse!

According to my diary, it was early evening when our dusty, mud-splattered bus pulled into Ceres. Joel had friends there, and they invited us to stay with them; ministry started almost right away. We held meetings in homes with a simple order of service: we led those who attended in some hymns, prayed, and gave short messages. Since my Portuguese was very limited, I thought Joel would take over the message part, but no, he insisted I preach, too! Some nights, Joel and I would sing duets, even when I did not know what I was singing: little by little, however, I began to pick up meaning! By day we'd visit friends of Joel's, and one day we visited friends of his from seminary who worked at the hospital and had a meal with them in the cafeteria.

Carl had asked us to visit Rubiataba, a small town, newly carved out of the surrounding forest, as were most of the villages in that area that we would visit. So, after a really good time of ministry in Ceres, on the 17th of January, we took off again by bus. It was a trip to be remembered!

The road to Ceres had been more like a superhighway in comparison to this one: dust and mud included. The road to Rubiataba was a real mess, mud, and water the whole way. At one point, after several attempts to get through an unusually bad place, the driver finally said, "Everyone get off the bus! You'll have to walk around this mud-hole."

And believe me, walking around the mud-hole was a challenge in itself!

We stood in awe as we watched the driver's tactics for going *through* the mud-hole. He proceeded to back up, paused to get his bearings, and then, full throttle, took a run at it! Will he get stuck, we wondered? But no! He made it! I had never seen anything like it: mud and water spraying in every direction, with the bus bouncing like a giant rubber ball! The bus driver? A rather handsome man, with black hair and a nicely trimmed mustache, took it all in his stride. At the door of the bus, he called to his open-mouthed passengers, "All aboard!" We obeyed and were soon on our way again.

Arriving in Rubiataba, we took in the quaintness of the village: almost all the houses had grass roofs and dirt-floors, no electricity, no running water. Joel and I looked up a small hotel, more like a bed and breakfast, known as a *pensão* in Portuguese. We were there from the 17th to the 22nd of January: a short but busy, fruitful, five days. During the day, we'd visit homes where we would tell people about salvation, reading to them from the Bible, and singing hymns for them. At night we held preaching services, and yes, with Joel's insistence, I did my part despite my broken Portuguese.

On the 22nd, a little after 9:00 in the morning, we left Rubiataba on foot, headed for another little town: Matazul. On the way, we spent the night at the home of a believer. My diary says nothing about our ministry in Matazul, but a lot about the night we spent on the way. You'll recall earlier how I declared I never learned to sleep in a hammock. Well, I did that night, battling dogs, cats, and mosquitos all night long!

Around 2:00 p.m. the following day we arrived in Matazul and went to the home of the local evangelist, who was also a friend of Joel's. That night, as usual, we held a preaching service.

On January 24th in Matazul I celebrated my 23rd birthday with newly-met members of the family of God, with little fanfare, a long way from friends and family: and from my fiancée Ebba!

Joel informed me it was time to start back on our evangelistic tour: this time to Crixas, farther yet into the interior. Joel borrowed some horses and saddles, and we left Matazul after lunch and started out on what would be a three-day trip across the hinterlands of the state of Goias. The first night we stayed at a farm where our hostess very graciously fed us a typical meal consisting of beans and rice, a meat (usually pork or chicken), with a fried egg on top! We had carried our hammocks behind our saddles, and once again I practiced hanging mine, almost as challenging as learning Portuguese, and managed to get a pretty good night's sleep.

We set off the next morning. It was the time of year, when everything was green, with wildflowers proliferating in the countryside; crystal-clear streams ran through the valleys. There were no real roads, however, just trails. It was easy to take the wrong one, which we did on one occasion.

It was very hot, and when we came to a stream or a river, we'd take a break, and bathe both ourselves and our horses. On one of these breaks, as we were bathing, a group of heavily armed men rode up. They began talking among themselves, looking our way, as though laying plans about whether to attack us, or to go on their way. We continued to bathe nonchalantly, hoping to give the appearance that we weren't a bit afraid of them, and after a while they rode away!

"They were no doubt bandits," Joel commented after they were gone, "and could easily enough have killed and robbed us of all we had. And who would have known the difference, out here in this deserted place."

Maybe he was right, but the Lord took care of us.

At the time, I knew nothing about Crixas, except that we were going there because it had no church or gospel witness. Some years later, however, after Ebba and I were married, we met a dear Christian lady who became our close friend. She shared with us that she had written a book of poems *about the founding of Crixas* where her grandmother had lived, and that it was from her that she had learned its history. Our friend's name was Sebastiana Ester Dietz de Oliveira. And her grandmother was Dona Francisca, who the townspeople affectionately called *Vo Chica* (Grandmother Francisca).

Not to get ahead of the story, but after arriving in Crixas, Joel and I stayed with Dona Francisca, our friend Sebastiana's grandmother! She loved to talk about her town with us, even as she had with her granddaughter, and let us know that the name Crixas came from Kirirás, a people group that roamed these jungles when the original Portuguese colonizers (*Bandeirantes*) arrived in Brazil many, many years ago.

It was the 27th of January when two very tired strangers on horseback rode into Crixas! People stared at us, probably more at me than at Joel. It was obvious that the white man with glasses was a stranger. There was no doubt about his coming from another part of the world, which was obvious because of how he spoke Portuguese. We were the talk of the town! We had been given the name of Dona Francisca and told that she was a woman in her 60's who had a room that she rented. She turned out to be a precious Christian woman!

Dona Francisca showed us to the room we would stay in. It was simply furnished, about seven feet wide and ten feet long. There was only one window with wooden shutters, a wooden door, and a dirt floor. The only decoration on the walls of our room was the skin of a jaguar that I had purchased from a man who ran a little store across the street from us. We rigged a way to hang our hammocks. Bats were plentiful, so at night, despite the heat, we covered every part of our bodies with a blanket. Some were vampire bats, thirsty for blood.

Settling in took no time at all, and that night we held the first of many preaching services in the small living room of Dona Francisca's house, with the light of small, kerosene-wicked lamps to read by. Our accommodation included board and room, with Dona Francisca providing all our meals.

I didn't know our hostess could not read when I gave her a can of margarine, which I thought would be a treat for her. After a while she came to me and confessed: *I don't know what this is. How do you open it?* The next time we gave her a can of peaches but opened it first. They found the fruit so delicious that they planted the seeds! Later someone told us they were puzzled why nothing had sprouted!

The Rio Vermelho flowed by the town of Crixas, about 150 yards from Dona Francisca's house: very convenient for washing our clothes. When we'd finished washing them, we'd spread them out to dry, and as we waited, we would pray together, and study our Bibles there beside the river.

We knew that everything we did was a novelty to the townspeople but had no idea that something as mundane as washing our clothes would have any significance for them. It wasn't until some twenty years later that I was told: "Whenever we saw you and Joel praying together and reading the Bible and talking about what you'd read down by the river, we thought what you were doing must be very important." No doubt, the longer we were there, they noticed something else: this white man with glasses was speaking Portuguese better every day!

It was 1952, but life in small towns like Crixas was more like something from the early nineteenth century: no electricity, running water, radios, post office, medical doctor, or hospital, with people who had never heard of canned goods. There were no roads, only trails for horses, ox carts or travel by foot.

Crixas had only three or four streets. At one end of the town square at the top of a hill stood the Roman Catholic Church. As incongruent as it sounds, a few feet beside it was the town jail. Outside of town, beyond the cemetery, was a landing strip on which only small planes could land although it was somewhat risky due to the slightly sloping terrain and tall trees at both ends of the airstrip.

Our ministry in Crixas took on a certain routine: either visiting homes or preparing for the evening meetings filled the daytime hours; and in the evening people gathered in Dona Francisca's living room to hear our messages, some with a sincere desire to learn more about God's Word, others out of curiosity. Both morning and evening activities had one purpose: to evangelize and reach hearts for Christ.

Of course, routines are made to be interrupted, and we had many interruptions: some things we could help with, others were outside our control. Where there are no doctors, missionaries often are called upon to help in medical emergencies. One day, I heard, "Come quickly, someone has drowned! We think he had a heart attack and fell into the river!"

I took off with the messenger to a house where they had carried the drowning victim. "Please, try to revive him," his friends and relatives pled!

Before I gave my life to serve the Lord by reaching the unreached with the gospel, I was planning to become a physician. Now, suddenly, I wished I had become a physician! But I did what I could. I set about checking his breathing, his heartbeat and pulse, and it didn't take long to determine I was too late to try artificial respiration.

Another medical emergency had to do with Sr. Antonio, who was chronically ill with what they felt was his liver, and I tended to agree. For certain, he was a very sick man. We had visited him on several different occasions.

Early one morning, someone came banging on our door, asking for us to go quickly to Antonio's house, screaming, "He's dying!" We threw on our clothes and took off running. When we got there, it was obvious to us that they were right! No doubt about it, Antonio was dying, and what a death: the poor man was twisting, groaning, grinding his teeth, and foaming at the mouth. A half hour after we had arrived, unable to do anything to help him, Antonio passed from this life into eternity. It was not a pretty sight, I assure you. Was he saved? Life and death are in God's hands: the hands of a God who is both merciful and gracious. I can say with assurance, that Antonio had heard the gospel message more than once, and that was a comfort to me.

His was my first experience with a Brazilian funeral. I helped to carry the simple, wooden casket from his home. As we walked through the town on the way to the cemetery, it seemed very strange to me that his wife did not follow along, but later I learned that this was the custom in that part of the country: wives did not watch the burial, which in some ways is more compassionate than how it's done in our own country.

The next interruption to our ministry routine had nothing to do with the people in Crixas. This time, it had to do with my co-worker Joel.: Unwelcome news arrived on March 11, 1952: Joel's father had passed away a month earlier. Joel started packing his things right away and sent them by ox cart to the town of *Itapaci*, sixty-five miles away. Shortly after, we left, too. Joel would travel with me as far as Goiania, where he would leave for Curitiba, in the state of Parana. And I would stay in Goiania with plans to eventually return to Crixas.

A local blacksmith, Oscar, was often hired to guide people, and we arranged for him to guide us to Itapaci. We left Crixas March 13th on the backs of burros! Oscar let us know what to expect: "To reach Itapaci, we'll have to climb over mountains, and there will be three rivers to cross. But once we reach Itapaci, things get easier. We'll be able to get a bus or truck from there on to Goiania. We'll cover 160 some miles in all."

We were well acquainted with the Rio Vermelho (*Red River*), where we washed our clothes, and that crossing was not difficult. The river was neither very wide nor deep. So, other than the time it would take, we were not very apprehensive about the other rivers. Little did we know what was ahead!

After several hours, plodding along on our donkeys, we came to a much larger river, the Rio Crixas, at flood-stage because of the heavy rains that had been falling for days.

Oscar called a halt and said, "Let me investigate things. I'm not sure we can cross. It's almost too swift right now to attempt it!"

He came back to us, and said, "The only thing we can do is wait it out!" And he went back to the river and pounded a stick in the sand at the water's edge. After an hour or so, he went back to examine the water level on the stick!

Returning to us, he said hesitantly, "I think I'll give it a try first on my own."

He made it across and back again, much to our relief. He told us, "I'm going to take one burro at a time." Which he did successfully and left them tied to a tree on the other side.

On his return, he brought a waterproof cape, large enough to cover both horse and rider in rainstorms. He spread the cape on the ground and then instructed us to take off all our clothes and put them on the cape. We looked at each other, shrugged our shoulders, and started undressing! All the rest of our gear, even my glasses, went next. It made a huge, heavy bundle, which he placed on his head, and waded out into the swirling, brown water, and proceeded toward the other side!

We stared after him, taking in the danger he was in! Bushes, limbs, and sometimes whole trees rushed downriver, making each of his crossings extremely dangerous. On this one, Oscar stepped into a hole and disappeared. Our hearts sank! There we stood, with no clothes on, wondering what we would do if he lost all our possessions! I'm sorry to admit, but my biggest concern was my glasses! When Oscar popped out of the water with the bundle, which was probably three feet in diameter, still on his head, we praised the Lord! Only God knows how he did it!

Last of all, Joel and I had to cross. This meant entering the water, cold water, and wading upriver, staying close to the edge until we could no longer find footing, and swimming with all our might toward the other bank. Joel did quite well, but I am not a strong swimmer, and before long, the current took me! In seconds, I was carried away. I probably went fifty yards before I could grasp bushes and grass along the opposite bank and manage to pull myself up out of the water. With a little chuckle, I told myself, "Alton, you just about didn't make it to your own wedding!"

Finally, we mounted our burros and were on our way again, fully dressed and I with my glasses anchored firmly on my nose. We stopped at a farm for the night, and the main subject of conversation with the people there was how near I came to drowning.

For the next three days we rode through rain, making it a miserable ride, and we couldn't stop thinking about the next river we had to cross. I told myself: *This crossing is NOT going to be like the last one!*

Though still out of sight, we knew when we were approaching the next river by the roar of the waters: scary! When it was in sight, it was worse than we had imagined. It was way over its banks, flooding large areas on both sides of the riverbed.

When Oscar and Joel discussed what we should do, I kept quiet, for I had already determined what I would or would not do! And my mind could not be changed: *this crossing was not going to be like the last*! After some serious deliberation, it was decided we would travel upriver till we reached a place where the river was narrow enough to cross safely.

After two days of traveling through rain, we found such a place, *and the crossing WAS NOT like the last!*

We came to a small village where we got a ride on a truck to take us to Rubiataba, and finally to Goiania. Our faithful, indefatigable guide Oscar left us at that point and returned to Crixas with the animals. During the years, he led many other such trips as ours, but on one of those, he died on the trail from a heart attack.

CHAPTER FOUR

BACK TO CRIXAS WITH JACK

*I*bid Joel goodbye in Goiania, and he continued with a heavy heart his journey to Curitiba to be with his family after the death of his father. Soon after, I found Joel's replacement, Jack Vaughn, who had been with me during our training at Fouts Springs, and had traveled down to Brazil with me on the MV Tribesman. I was happy when Jack agreed to go back to Crixas with me.

But prior to my return to Crixas, some rather interesting opportunities came my way. They began with Carl Taylor inviting me to go with him to visit some of the new towns that were springing up in the interior of the state of Goias, quite a distance from Goiania. Carl's friend, Dr. Borba, owned some land in the area. On April 8, 1952, Carl and I climbed into the cab of Dr. Borba's truck, loaded with people and supplies in the back. The countryside was beautifully lush and green, but farther into the interior, despite the beauty of the countryside, the roads were not very good!

Very late that first night, we arrived at the historic town of Goias, the first capital of that state. We checked into a room in a small hotel, weary and needing a good night's rest. Early the next morning, we started out again, arriving in Jussara around noon, which was a very hot time of day!

In the evening, we held a preaching service at the hotel where we spent the night. Interest and response to the Gospel were good, and in my diary, I recorded: *one man was saved.* The three days we were in Jussara we had many opportunities to visit with people and to share the message of salvation, which was the reason for the trip. Every night Carl and I held meetings at the hotel. On the fourth day of our evangelistic trip, we returned to Goiania.

The next opportunity that came my way was in Pontalina, another small town in the southern part of Goias, where a small church had already been established. Jack Vaughn had been living there for a time with his Brazilian companion, John, to perfect his Portuguese and to gain experience in using it to communicate the gospel, as I had done in Crixas.

Bill Price flew me to Pontalina in the mission's four-place Stinson on April 16th. As we approached the village, Bill buzzed the street that ran through the center of town to clear it of people, dogs, cattle, and anything else that could pose a danger upon landing. Making sure of that, he circled once again, finally landing on the airstrip at the end of the street, stirring up a terrible cloud of dust. The plane became the center of attraction: kids and adults watched everything we did. That very night we held a service in the little Presbyterian church.

The following day, Carl Taylor and his family arrived on the bus from Goiania.

Gypsies traveled about the countryside on horses, living in tents. They had set up a temporary encampment outside Pontalina. One afternoon, Jack and I decided to visit their camp to share the Gospel with them. We were well received and broke the ice by playing hymns on an old-fashioned Victrola that played 78 RPM records. Of course, the Gypsy ladies wanted to read our palms and tell our fortunes. We knew it was how they earned their money, but we respectfully declined. By sharing Jesus with them, however, we were telling their fortunes—we were letting them know that their futures depended on placing their faith in Him.

The day after the Taylors arrived in Pontalina, Bill Price flew Carl and me over to Crominia, a few minutes away by plane. We landed in a field on the edge of town, and were surrounded by dozens of curious townspeople wondering why we had come. They were soon to find out. There, beside the plane, we gave out tracts and began witnessing.

Carl was so impressed with the interest and response we'd received, that he said, "You know, Alton, I think you should stay here for a week and do some visitation and preaching!"

"Okay," I said, a bit taken aback. And it wasn't until Carl and Bill took off on the plane that I began to realize how ill-prepared I was. I had only the clothes on my back, no razor or toothbrush, just a little money in my pocket, and my Portuguese New Testament.

I began walking into town with the crowd, and learned on the way that there was no church. "But there are a few people who believe like you here and there on nearby farms," someone told me. Soon the people went on their way. I didn't know a soul, but then, God brought a young believer named Paulo to befriend me.

For the next few days, I stayed in a *pensão* (establishment that offered board and room). And Paulo and I became a team. We visited in homes during the day, and at night, we held open-air street meetings, singing and preaching the Good News of Salvation by faith in Jesus.

I shared Ephesians 2:8-9 at one of these street meetings. *"For by grace are you saved through faith; and that not of yourselves: it is the gift of God: not of works, lest anyone should boast."*

I tried to illustrate salvation being *a gift*. I held up my New Testament and thought I was saying: "If I were to offer this New Testament as a gift, what would you have to do to get it?" I was hoping someone would say, "If it was a gift, all I would have to do would be to take it."

A man standing in the back thought I'd said, "Who wants this New Testament as a gift?" And he came right up and said, "I'll take it!"

It was the only New Testament I had with me, and for the rest of the meetings, I had to borrow a Bible! But when I get to heaven, I'll learn what happened to the man who had my testament. Hopefully, I'll be told he took Jesus just as eagerly as he took my New Testament.

When my week in Crominia was finished, much work had been done and I was ready to get back to Goiania. Bill Price flew Cora Taylor and their children back to Goiania, but Carl and I took the 150-mile bus trip over bumpy, dusty roads: certainly not a comfortable ride, but intensely interesting!

Other than mentioning earlier that Ebba had been placed in a Brazilian home to learn Portuguese, I've left her out of the story thus far. So, to bring her back in, Ebba lived with a Brazilian doctor and his family. Dr. José Peixoto da Silveira and his wife Dona Galiana had several children who soon learned to love Ebba. (Ahem! What's not to love?) Ebba's job as an *au pair* was to teach the children English as she polished her Portuguese. Ebba soon became one of the family, and Dona Galiana and Dr. José were proud of their American "daughter." It was with them that Ebba learned to make and serve, among other things, the famous Brazilian *cafezinho:* sweet, strong coffee, always served in a demitasse cup. Ebba stayed with this family until we were married. Dr. José was Secretary of Health for the state of Goias at the time and was deeply involved in politics. He held various offices over the years, even running for governor once.

Anytime I was in Goiania, I'd spend as much time as I could with Ebba, usually in the evenings. When it was by day, we would often visit Brazilian friends or other missionaries. Since Ebba was treated as a daughter in the Silveira family, we were both eager to maintain the highest moral standards in their home. Ebba would not even sit on the same sofa with me when I went to see her, and I would sit (reluctantly) across the room from her. Later, we realized that such an extreme measure was not necessary, nor expected. Usually, I would bring her chocolates. A couple of times, I arrived at the house, only to find no one at home. Humm! I wasn't too happy about that!

At times, I asked myself if I really wanted to marry this girl. She tried to explain to me that she hadn't meant to break the date, but wherever the family went, she was expected to go along. Anyway, she didn't think it proper to be alone with me in the house. Once, when she had stood me up, I walked a few blocks to a park near the capitol building, sat on a bench, and ate the chocolates *all by myself*. Pouting? What do you think?

During the time I was in Crixas, Ebba was ill with hepatitis, and had to spend a few weeks in bed. She'd been helping other missionaries who had contracted the disease, and had probably picked it up from them. But she was in good hands at Silveira's.

During that first year in Brazil, I could usually be found ministering in small towns, but when I returned to Goiania from Crixas to bring Joel out, I was asked to do something entirely different. The city of Vianopolis donated a parcel of ground to the mission on which to build a boarding school for the children of NTM missionaries. Clayton and Nina Templeton, with whom I took missionary training, were overseeing the work. In April, Clayton asked me to join him in Vianopolis to build bunk beds and desks: things vital for any boarding school. I have no idea if my handy work has endured this long or has had to be replaced, but the school is no longer functioning. It served several generations of missionaries' children. For many years, the city of Vianopolis was also the headquarters of what became known as *Missão Novas Tribos do Brasil*.

In May, Jack Vaughn and I started purchasing and packing what we'd need to take with us to Crixas, but I made time to be with Ebba as much as I could and helped her with some of the things we'd need for our soon-coming wedding.

On May 11th, Bill Price weighed our supplies, Jack and I loaded them into the Stinson, and soon, we were in the air headed for Crixas. All went well for the first part of the trip, but then we couldn't locate Crixas from the air and were running short on gasoline. We were glad for a level-headed pilot who told us, "We're going to have to go back to Ceres, land there and try again tomorrow."

We took off early the next morning, and following landmarks, we located the little airstrip in the pasture just outside of Crixas. Bill made two trips from Ceres to Crixas that day to get all our things to us.

Once in Crixas, Jack and I followed the same routine that Joel and I had established. During the day we took care of correspondence, washed our clothes, and visited people in their homes. Each night, we took turns preaching in Dona Francisca's tiny living room (near to the spare room we rented from her).

Because of all the seed that had been planted previously in Crixas, Jack and I harvested souls right away, which is proof that Isaiah 55:11 is true: "*So shall my word be that goes forth out of my mouth: it shall not return unto me void, but it shall accomplish that which I please, and it shall prosper in the thing whereto I sent it.*"

May 21st: five people were saved, a girl and four adults.

June 8th: another five people confessed their faith in Jesus.

June 9th: Senhor Zilo and Dona Eva both accepted the Lord.

We had heard that Dona Eva was a strong Roman Catholic, and was not likely to receive us into her home. But we prayed before going to her house. God had prepared her heart! Not only did she ask us in, but she was very gracious and welcoming.

"Come in," she said, "my husband is not here, but tell *me* about the Bible."

We answered the questions she had and explained to her "*There is only one mediator between God and man, the Man Christ Jesus.*" When we asked her if she would like to be saved and to know that she would go to heaven when she died, she answered in the affirmative, and took Jesus as her Savior! Just then Senhor Zilo walked in, and we proceeded to explain salvation to him and invited him to put his faith in Christ. And he did. Dona Eva remained a faithful believer until she died many years later.

I met Pedro Dietz's sons in Crixas, John and Joaquim, and became good friends with them. When their father Pedro came to Brazil from Holland, he heard about a location near Crixas rich with gold, and that was how he happened to settle there, and that's where his sons grew up. Both were merchants at the time I met them, as well as being involved in politics. Joaquim's wife, Dona Honoria, was one of the first fruits of my ministry in that village. Joaquim found the Lord later and became an elder in the Crixas Presyterian Church. Over the years, Crixas grew, and became a city, and Joaquim was elected mayor two different times. (There is more to the Dietz story, so, to quote Paul Harvey, *tune in for the rest of the story, a little farther along in the book.*)

The more my Portuguese improved, the more interesting the opportunities were that came my way. I began to feel 'at home' in Crixas, and knew that the townspeople were beginning to warm up to me as well.

One day a couple came to visit me, carrying a small baby, and what happened next was reminiscent of Matthew 19:14: *"Jesus said, 'Let the little children come to me, and to not stand in their way, for the kingdom of heaven belongs to such as these."* We visited for a while before they let me know the reason for their visit. They knew that I wouldn't baptize their baby, but asked, "Will you dedicate our baby to the Lord?"

"Of course, I will!" I responded. I took baby Daniel in my arms. We bowed our heads and asked the Lord to watch over him, and that his parents would be faithful to bring him up to love the Lord. (And as with the Dietz brothers, there is more to Daniel's story: *stay tuned.*)

As the number of believers grew, so did their curiosity about God's Word. The Lord laid it upon my heart to not only evangelize, but to teach the chronology of the Bible: God's dealings with Israel, the church age, and end times. I remembered how charts and other visual aids had helped me to get a handle on when events in the Bible took place, or would take place in the future, and I tried to produce a chart for the growing church in Crixas.

I purchased some stiff white cloth at one of the little stores in town, located some colored pencils, and, remembering the things included in the charts that had helped me to grow spiritually, I sketched and colored a dispensational chart. It turned out to be quite a project, but when I presented it in the nightly meetings, I had a very interested audience. I knew I was about to leave them, and wanted them to have a foundation upon which to build as they studied their Bibles.

Jack and I continued our routines: daily washing our clothes, bathing, praying by the river, studying for evening messages, and having Bible studies with individuals. It paid off! The opportunities we had to share the message of salvation seemed endless. And one more person was saved on June 18th!

In a few more weeks I'd be leaving Crixas. I'd be with Ebba, and we'd be firming up plans for a wedding that would take place on July 25, 1952: a wedding that was a long-time-coming for a certain young groom.

My heart was both joyous and sad those last few days in Crixas. I looked forward to seeing Ebba, the love of my life, but I'd be saying goodbye to people that I'd become very attached to, especially those who had put their faith in Christ. Jack and I couldn't help but wonder how many would continue to follow the Lord? Would this infant church plant grow and expand?

We'd let Bill Price know we needed a flight out on June 26th. He scheduled it for late afternoon, and let us know that because of the short airstrip and the weight (all negative factors) he wouldn't be able to take us both out at the same time.

Early afternoon on the 26th, we began carrying our things out to the airstrip, weighed and ready to go, and waited for Bill to arrive. We spotted the plane circling the town, chasing off the animals that might hinder his landing, and then, with precision, he brought the plane down. He helped us load our things, and then told us: "I'll be taking Jack first. And since I'll have to take off down-wind, it's going to be difficult to clear the tall trees at the bottom end of the pasture. I'm going to need as much runway as possible, so help me drag the plane to the upper end of the field, and into the woods and brush as far as we can go."

Once the plane was in position, Jack got in first, and Bill made sure his seat belt was safely latched, before hurrying to the other side, and taking his seat behind the controls. Bill gunned the motor, released the brake, and the plane took off down the runway, picking up speed. I watched, with bated breath! Would Bill get the plane in the air before hitting the trees at the other end of the field? When he cleared the trees

by a narrow margin, I let my breath out with a big sigh, and whispered:
only with God's help!

I waited there on the strip for my turn, not forgetting for one minute
how close a call it had been, and wondered at the courage it took to be a
missionary pilot who faced all kinds of risks daily to keep us missionaries
at our jobs.

Two or three hours later, Bill returned for me. I waited as he latched
me in, thinking *it'll be easier, we're lighter now,* but as we cleared the
treetops at the end of the airfield, I caught myself letting my breath out,
just the same!

Maintaining correspondence during the months Ebba and I were
apart was erratic, to say the least, with me in the backwoods of Crixas
and Ebba in the bustling city of Goiania! I wrote a lot of letters to her,
some by hand and some on my little portable manual typewriter. Since
there was no post office, I could only send letters out when someone was
going on foot or horseback. On her end, Ebba was lovingly and faithfully
writing me every day and sending her letters to Itapaci or Rubiataba.
There they stayed in the post office until someone going to Crixas would
take the accumulation of mail on horseback or by ox cart. Many times I
would receive from ten to thirty letters at a time. Of course I devoured
them (well, not really), but they were wonderful to receive. Ebba used
to include clippings of a cartoon known as 'The Tiger's Friend' (*Amigo
da Onça*), taken from a weekly news magazine. The cartoons were funny
and always depicted something from everyday Brazilian life, usually with
irony. Years later, the man who made everyone laugh with his cartoons,
committed suicide. Sad! I used to tell Ebba I never bothered to read all
those letters, but they came in handy for starting fires! That, however,
was anything but the truth!

The slowness of sending and receiving mail, however, made it hard to work together on making plans for our wedding!

Thus ended my time in Crixas. When I left, I had no idea that it would be twenty-one years before the next chapter involving Crixas would be enacted. Little did I realize what wonders would take place in the lives of many people in that out-of-the-way village during those twenty-one years.

CHAPTER FIVE

WEDDING BELLS

I had adjusted to living in small towns and traveling in the forests of the interior of Brazil, by donkeys, horses, and *shank's pony!* The cuisine was simple, predictable, but I'd come to enjoy whatever was prepared by the kind women who hosted us on farms as we traveled, and in the towns where we served. It was amazing, even to myself, how much Portuguese I gained while interacting with Joel: a wonderful teacher and trainer in ministry, who showed me how to reach hearts for Christ in out-of-the-way places. I'll always be indebted to him. And to Carl Taylor, who engaged Joel to be my partner.

Carl had done the same thing for Ebba: putting her in contact with people in Goiania who took her into their home as a part of their family. While I was out roughing it, she was learning the culture and the more sophisticated type of Portuguese spoken in the cities. And so it was, that when we were about to be married, God had given us so many tools we could use as a couple wherever he planned to use us in Brazil.

It is true that *absence makes the heart grow fonder!* And when we were reunited at last, we were more than ready for Wedding Bells to ring!

A bride's gown is for her of first importance! God met that need through two people: Ebba's mother, who couldn't come for the wedding, purchased a beautiful gown and sent it to her daughter via Carl Taylor, who 'just happened' to be in the States on mission business. I wish I could describe the dress for my female readers, but all I can say is, it took my breath away when Ebba came down the aisle!

The groom's suit is not so important to him, but to the bride, is also of utmost importance. So, one of the first things I did when I came out of the interior and reached Goiania, was to look for a tailor. He took my measurements and Ebba helped me decided on a style and color, which was blue.

The rings, costly for just-starting-out missionaries, were provided by my parents, who couldn't be there to see us slipping them on each other's fingers! Carl brought them to us along with the gown. The rings were too large, but they arrived in time to have them sized and ready for the wedding ceremony. When you think of how long we wore those rings (almost 65 years), they really got a *workout.*

The preacher was an easy choice. Clayton and Nina Templeton had gone through training with us in Fouts Springs. I'd gotten to know and appreciate Clayton as we travelled together to meetings where we represented NTM: I sang, he preached! We'd shared many good times together on the boat to Brazil, as well. There was no one else we could think of that we'd rather have to perform our wedding ceremony.

At this stage, since there was so much to get done, Ebba and I had divided up who would do what! Since Templeton's weren't in Goiania, but in Vianopolis at the school for missionaries' children, it was decided that I would travel there to confer with Clayton concerning the order of service and other things pertinent to our becoming one. Since Clayton had been a pastor and had done other weddings, he had a lot of good suggestions!

Maid of Honor and Best Man? Again, easy! Delbert (Duffy) and Madeline Denelsbeck meant a lot to us, and were honored to stand up with us. It worked out that they would also provide us the honeymoon housing!

Duffy invited me to go with him to Barra do Garças, in the state of Mato Grosso where he had been building a house with the intention of reaching tribes along the Araguaia River. Because of health problems, however, they had to leave Barra do Garças and work in Goiania, but Duffy wanted my company when he went to check on the house, which was on the Mato Grosso side of the river. We were there for four days, and while there, we helped in the little Presbyterian Church.

Naturally Duffy and I talked about our coming wedding, and he was happy to accept being my Best Man, and said, "Well, Alton, I'll do more than that! How about you bring your bride to our house here for your honeymoon!" And I was happy to accept his offer, as well.

After we returned to Goiania, I had no idea how to get a marriage license. I went to the office where all kinds of legal documents are issued (called the *cartório*). The official in charge is called the *escrivão*. I asked this official, "What do I need to get married?" His answer made me chuckle: "You need a girl willing to marry you."

"Oh, I already have the girl!" I returned quickly.

"Oh, well, then," he said, "the rest is easy! Bring your bride and witnesses, and I'll do the rest."

Things were starting to line up! Carl Taylor arrived back in Brazil on July 21st, just four days before the wedding. The gown he'd brought fit Ebba like a glove! The rings were too big, as I've already said, but "Not to worry," the jeweler told us, "I'll have them ready on time!" And he did.

On July 24, Ebba and I, Duffy and Madeline, and a few others walked to the *cartório* for the civil ceremony, required in Brazil. The *escrivão* loudly read all the words of the legal wedding certificate to everyone present. We signed our names, and we were legally married! As we walked out the door, I said: "I sure hope I feel more married tomorrow than I do right now!" We had a good laugh, and walked home! (Me a little taller! Prouder!)

"Oh, no, flowers! Ebba told me she wanted roses for the wedding," I remembered as I walked by a yard filled with rose bushes. "I think I'll see if I could have some of these!" I boldly knocked on the door. When a lady opened it, I got right to the point, "I just noticed your beautiful roses. I'm getting married tomorrow. Do you suppose you could give me some of them?"

"I'll make sure you'll have roses for your bride!" she told me. "Where will the wedding take place?" She didn't tell me the rest of what she was planning, which was to recruit some friends to add the roses in their yards to hers!

The next morning, the day of our wedding, Jack Vaughn and I set out on bicycles to collect the roses. We returned to the lady's house, whose name I didn't even know, and after picking up her roses, she sent us to other houses where more roses were awaiting us! We took them all back to the First Baptist Church of Goiania where the marriage would take place, and set about decorating the church. We had more than enough. The church was fragrant and beautiful when people began to show up! Some of the ladies whose roses were in full display attended our wedding!

July 25, 1952, the date that had *seemed* so far away when it was first set, was finally here! The wedding would begin at two in the afternoon, and everything seemed to be going according to schedule!

Jack and I were staying in a small hotel, along with others from our mission family who had come for the wedding. A taxi had been chartered to take us all to the church. Of course, several trips had to be made, and Jack and I would be picked up last. For some unknown reason, the taxi didn't come back for us. We waited and waited, but at 1:30, we took off running for the center of town, where we could find another taxi to take us the rest of the way. We arrived at the church with just a few minutes to spare, hot and sweaty! But the ceremony started on time.

I was waiting at the front with Duffy and Clayton, watching the Maid of Honor coming down the aisle, and then, Ebba came on the arm of Clem Smith. I was glad that Jack sang his song first. I had to catch my breath again after seeing my beautiful bride!

I'd chosen to sing the song that I'd heard at other weddings, but at those, my mind wandered to other things: the voice of the singer, and what they were wearing! Today, I wasn't just listening; I was pouring out my heart to the one I loved with lyrics that described my sentiments exactly. Whenever I'd sung songs before, it was to an audience. This time it was to someone very special. So, forgetting the people gathered in the church, I looked at Ebba and sang:

Because, you come to me,
With naught save love,
And hold my hand and lift mine eyes above,
A wider world of hope and joy I see,
Because you come to me!

Because you speak to me in accent sweet,
I find the roses waking 'round my feet,
And I am led through tears and joy to thee,
Because you speak to me!

__Because__ God made thee mine,
I'll cherish thee,
Through light and darkness through all time to be,
And pray His love may make our love divine,
Because God made thee mine
(Nicholas Brodszky-lyrics by Sammy Cahn)

The wedding went very well, I'm told, but I'm afraid I can't remember much, if anything at all, about what Clayton said in his exhortations to us. I recall others saying the same about their weddings.

There were both English and Portuguese speakers in attendance, but Clayton addressed his message to us in English, our heart language at the time. When he gave permission for me to kiss the bride, I did! Ebba had to practically push me away.

After the wedding, there was a reception at Carl and Cora Taylor's home on Street 55. It was held in the front yard. As the festivities went on, we noticed kids from the neighborhood sitting on the brick walls around the yard to take it all in. I'm sure we gave them quite a show! There was finger food (*salgados*) and a nice cake. At the end, I followed tradition and carried my bride across the threshold into Carl's house, a sign that the newlyweds were about to take off on their honeymoon.

It was late afternoon, we changed into other clothes, and smiling as we exited the house, we waved goodbye, got into a taxi, which would take us to the 'Hotel Comercial' in the city of Anapolis, where we stayed for two days, in the lap of luxury, as I saw it, having so recently been living in the humble dwellings of the interior of Brazil.

Our original plan was to have Bill Price fly us to São Lourenco, a resort city in the state of Minas Gerais, but he had to cancel the flight when his wife became ill.

We returned to Goiania, and on the 29th, with his wife much improved, Bill flew us to Aragarças where we could stay in Denelsbeck's home for as long as we wished. Since their house was on the other side of the river, we crossed the river in a small boat, since no bridge existed at that time: somehow that seemed romantic. Bill crossed with us and helped us carry our things to the house. Upon opening the door, a couple of bats flew at us! You can't imagine Ebba's reaction to this! Or can you? Bill said his goodbyes, and there we were! Mr. and Mrs. Alton Cothron having a dream honeymoon, on my part, for every time Ebba was startled by creepy crawlies, she flew into my arms! She had never heard a donkey bray: a horrible, indescribable sound to someone who has no idea what is causing it! Only this time, instead of into my arms, Ebba almost dived under the bed!

Our three weeks in the little village of Barra do Garças were wonderful. Ebba and I also attended and helped in the small Presbyterian church and soon got to know people with whom we enjoyed fellowshipping. In the evenings, we'd dress up in our wedding attire, play Monopoly, and eat popcorn, enjoying being *just the two of us!* Sometimes people came to see us. One day we hiked to a beautiful waterfall not far from where we were staying.

The town on the other side of the river had a powerful loudspeaker, still a common thing in small interior towns in Brazil, over which music is played every night. Two songs were repeated night after night for our benefit, we think, since they were in English: 'Easter Parade' and 'Jezebel.' The sound carried for miles, it seemed. So many times since then, we have reminisced about the fun we had on our honeymoon, and have laughed about mixing our formal attire with a mundane game of Monopoly, while crunching popcorn!

The day came when we had to leave. This was prompted, in part, by the fact that Ebba had an apparent appendicitis attack on the night of August 20th. (A few months later, she had surgery to solve this problem.) We locked the house, took our things, crossed the river, and went to the airport, where we got on a National Airline flight to Goiania.

We were so young! Sometimes people would ask us if we were siblings! And when we told them we were married, they thought we were pulling their legs!

After the wedding, we went to a studio for pictures. When we returned from the honeymoon, we were anxious to see how they'd turned out. The photos turned out fine and we were pleased with that aspect, but I almost fainted when I saw what I owed! And I asked, "Why did you make so many?" They showed us the paperwork, and then we understood, much to my embarrassment, I had confused the size of the picture with the price, resulting in so many pictures. We wondered who we could give them all to. I paid for them, worrying about how we would eat until our next allowance check came from the mission, but not to worry! Loving colleagues came to our rescue and made sure we didn't go hungry. Eventually, I got over the shock of what they'd cost, and we laughed about it for years even after we were old and only faintly resembled the young couple smiling up at us from their *wedding photograph*.

CHAPTER SIX

LANGUAGE SCHOOL

*S*everal of us from NTM applied to a language school in *Campinas, São Paulo,* geared toward missionaries and businesspeople. The school offered classes based upon memorizing frequently used phrases, learning areas of meaning for words we already knew, and increasing our vocabularies, all with an emphasis on pronunciation and inflection of voice. After memorizing, the next step was to bring what was memorized up to speed so that the student learned to converse without hesitation. The course usually took a year to complete. (But some of us who had already acquired a working knowledge of Portuguese by in-country immersion, were able to complete the course in six months.)

The group that applied to the language school from NTM consisted of Jack Vaughn, the Cothrons, Stahls, and Lyle Denelsbecks. Our acceptance letters arrived, and we were overjoyed! Of course, they informed us that we would need to arrange our own places of residence. Which we did, thanks to the Presbyterian Mission. They owned a house in Campinas, that would be torn down soon to make room for a highway. While it was standing, they told us we could live there free of charge. It was large enough to accommodate our whole group: a great help financially! There were plenty of bedrooms, but we'd share the kitchen.

We wasted no time getting on our way. Our acceptance letters arrived on the 26th, and on the 28th of August, we left Goiania aboard a Cruzeiro do Sul Airplane, headed for Campinas. Jack, Ebba, and I were comfortable in Portuguese already, but the Stahls and Denelsbecks were just beginning their study of the language.

The Denelsbecks had a kerosene refrigerator, which they kindly shared with the rest of us. Each couple and Jack were assigned a small corner of it. We were very compatible and had lots of fun together, which sometimes came with playing tricks on each other!

Ebba and I had prepared our meal, carried it into the dining room right off the kitchen, and sat down. We bowed our heads, joined hands, and reverently engaged in prayer, unhurriedly thanking God for several things. We squeezed each other's hand when the 'Amen' was pronounced, opened our eyes, and exclaimed to no one in particular, "Where's our food!"

We heard the ill-concealed laughter of our co-students in the kitchen! While we prayed, they quietly confiscated our dinner!

Couples learn from one another, especially living together in such close quarters. I was challenged by Lyle Denelsbeck's good example. While his wife was in classes, he would bake things for her. One afternoon, I asked Lyle, "How about teaching me how to follow a recipe, and I'll make a cake for Ebba."

"Sure," he said, and patiently showed me how to go about it. The cake turned out nice, so nice that I decided to share it! By the time Ebba came home from her classes, there was only one piece left! (She really wasn't that impressed!)

One of the first things I did was to make some simple cupboards for our food and other supplies. I bought the tools I would need and some light lumber, thinking, *I can disassemble the cupboards, and use the lumber for crating material when we leave for the state of Rio Grande do Sul where we'll be working with the Kaingang in southern Brazil."* I am always thinking ahead! Perhaps it was acquired by living with practical parents, or something I learned from our earlier training in Fouts Springs; probably a little of both.

While in Campinas, Ebba and I made it a point to attend church services in the Portuguese language. On weekends, the group of us would go to outlying suburbs to hold street meetings, do home visitation, and preach to whoever would listen. We were all kept busy with language lessons, but we found it important to balance our studies with times of relaxation. Picnics in a nearby park was one of our favorite outings. But the things we did that had to do with ministry were also enjoyable and gave us ways to practice what we were learning.

The director of Youth for Christ, Don Phillips, invited us to participate in meetings with Brazilian young people. Jack Vaughn and I joined up with Harold Reimer, who later became the director of Word of Life in Brazil, to form a men's trio. Soon, we were singing in churches all over Campinas and in other cities: some so far afield that we had overnight stays in hotels. Once, when Ebba accompanied us and we were checking into a hotel, the clerk looked at us askance when we told him we needed one room. To him, we looked too young to be a married couple!

We took a break from our studies and, on November 18th, left Campinas by train for Goiania to attend our mission's second Field Conference, feeling like old-timers since we'd also attended the first. An old, wood-burning steam engine pulled the train. If you opened the window in the passenger car, you were likely to have sparks and hot coals land in your lap or hair. It was hot, and you needed the air, but when you tired of slapping out the sparks, you'd close it, and then you'd begin the process all over again when you couldn't stand the heat any longer. It was well worth the uncomfortable ride, however, once we arrived in Goiania and were with friends and colleagues again. Thanksgiving fell during the conference, and we all went to a park for a picnic to celebrate it: somewhat nostalgic for *home!*

The conference ended, and we traveled back to Campinas to resume language study on December 1st. The suspicion of an inflamed appendix had interrupted our honeymoon, but on the morning of December 13th the suspicion became a reality, and at 11 in the morning, Ebba underwent an appendectomy in a nearby hospital. She was discharged from the hospital five days later. It was the first time we were separated since being married! It did set Ebba back some in her studies, but she quickly caught up!

Ruskin Garber, director of NTM, was visiting Brazil to see firsthand how things were going on this new field and to acquire information concerning tribal people in Brazil that were still unreached with the Gospel. He made a trip to Campinas in December to meet with those of us in language study. For several days, he laid out before us needs that we might consider filling, sharing with us all he had gleaned in his travels about the field. It was at that time that Ebba and I felt God leading us to work with the Kaingang.

Our good friends, Abe Koop and Dee Bleigh, were married at the end of December and invited us to join them in Rio de Janeiro for their honeymoon. We took a bus to Rio on the 31st, and the Koops and Cothrons celebrated their first New Year's Eve together as married couples in Rio de Janeiro, Brazil! We stayed with Abe and Dee for three days, taking in all the attractions of that famous city, including Sugar Loaf Mountain, the huge statue of Christ (*Corcovado*), and the beaches. It was so much fun comparing and sharing our romances and weddings!

During all the years we lived in Brazil we had only two real vacations, and Rio de Janeiro was the first!

It was a nice break, but we hurried back to Campinas and really applied ourselves to our studies for another month, and on February 28th, classes ended for Ebba and me, who were now much better equipped to minister in Portuguese! We began packing for the next big phase of our life and ministry in Brazil!

CHAPTER SEVEN

SURVEY OF THE KAINGANG RESERVATIONS

---

*D*uring our time in Goiania for the second Field Conference, we met up with Floyd and Ida Gilbert. Floyd and his family lived in Belem, but when he discovered he had tuberculosis, his doctor told him, "I can treat you in Belem, but the hot, humid climate here will make a cure more difficult. I recommend that you move to Goiania, where the climate is much more conducive to recovery from tuberculosis." So, they pulled up roots and moved to Goiania for a much better climate.

By the time we met the Gilberts in Goiania, Floyd was much improved and had itchy feet to get back to work. Like us, he was still trying to find God's guidance concerning where to put his hand to the plough! He began going to the city library and researching tribal peoples in Brazil and their locations. Like other missionaries, he thought all tribal groups existed only in the Amazon basin of Brazil. Much to his surprise, he found that other groups existed in the savannahs and forests in the south of Brazil, such as the Guarani and the Kaingang. Not only do they exist at the present time, but they were in existence when European colonists first landed in Brazil in the 1500s, bringing with them the Portuguese language.

One day during the Field Conference, Floyd shared his findings with me and said, "Alton, I'd like to do a survey of the Kaingang tribe in the southern parts of Brazil. This might be an unreached tribe that is reachable, in that no contact work needs to be done, since they are already living on reservations bordering cities and towns and are not hostile to outsiders! I'd sure like it if you'd join me in the survey."

Floyd had given Ebba and me food for thought. We added prayer to our thinking when we returned to finish our language study in Campinas. After Rus Garber's visit, we let Floyd know that we'd help with the survey.

Floyd had recovered from tuberculosis and had moved his family to the city of Ponta Grossa, in the state of Parana, closer to where the survey would take place. A Christian man in Ponta Grossa, Theofolo Brephol, kindly provided a small, simple wooden house for them to live in: rent free!

On March 7, 1953, soon after we finished our six-month language course in Campinas, Ebba and I flew from São Paulo to Ponta Grossa, excited to be launching into partnership with our dear friends, the Gilberts!

"If you don't mind tight quarters," Floyd told us, "You can live with us rent-free!"

We couldn't turn down an offer like that! Then, we saw the room we would live in—so small you had to walk sideways between the bed and the wall. When we were alone, Ebba looked things over and pleaded, "I think we had better buy a mattress, Alton."

I shook my head in the affirmative, looked Floyd up, and we set out to hunt for one! We found a store that carried bedroom furnishings.

Though I hadn't been in Brazil very long, one thing I had already learned was that prices in Brazil are always subject to negotiation. So, I went to work on the salesman to lower the price of the mattress of my choice. I must be a good bargainer, for the man lowered the price so much I was ashamed *not* to buy it! It turned out to be a comfortable mattress, and it went with us wherever we moved for many years.

Recalling how my friend, Lyle Denelsbeck, showed his love for his wife by baking, I decided to refresh my culinary talents to impress my wife with how much I loved her. The cake I made under Lyle's tutelage while in language school turned out so good that I set to work in the Gilbert's kitchen to make another of the same recipe. Before I started, Ebba said, "Be sure to keep the egg whites. I know a recipe for making a good frosting, but it takes two egg whites."

"Will do!" I answered. The cake turned out as nice as the first one, and I was quite proud of myself. "Here's the cake, Ebba. I'll turn the frosting part over to you!"

"Where's the egg whites?" she asked.

"Egg *whites*?" I asked, handing her a cup with two yolks! "I'll be right back." And I took off for a nearby neighborhood store to buy two more eggs! We were dirt poor at the time, but we enjoyed the beautifully frosted cake when it was ready despite the added expense!

One evening, we were all getting ready for church. I was dressed in my suit and tie and had gone out in the backyard to brush my teeth. It was already dark at the time. Ida Gilbert opened the kitchen door and threw out a basin of dishwater, which caught me squarely in the face! I jumped and yelled, after the fact, but the damage was done! (The house did not have plumbing, and our dish pans were large!) Ida was horrified, of course, and I was soaked, but soon, we were both laughing!

When our preparations for the survey trip and our itinerary were finished, we let our wives know that we'd probably be gone for a couple of weeks. We bid them and the Gilbert children farewell and took off for the city of Curitiba, the capital of the state of Paraná.

We didn't want to have trouble along the way, so as soon as we arrived in Curitiba, we looked up the office of the Regional Director of the Indian Protective Service. Without any trouble, we obtained written permission to visit all the reservations in southern Brazil. While the government had little or no interest in our preaching the Gospel, it was happy for any material or social help we might give the people on the reservations.

The official that we spoke to explained to us that the Kaingang were considered an *integrated tribe* by the government agency, meaning that it was losing its culture and language and absorbing much of the Brazilian language and culture.

Not to get ahead of things, but from the survey, we ascertained the following: most of the Kaingang men speak some Portuguese, many of them quite well, but the women and children, for the most part, spoke only their native language. Some still hunted with bows and arrows, but most used firearms. They were now wearing clothing, and planting crops such as corn, beans, and wheat, and raising pigs and chickens for their own consumption.

Syncretism describes their religion. They had retained some of their native beliefs, but these beliefs were heavily sprinkled with Roman Catholic religious customs. Those who spoke Portuguese, except for a few, spoke a mixture of the two languages: Kaingang and Portuguese, another form of syncretism.

The causes of death among their children were generally complications from the common cold, pneumonia, dysentery, or malnutrition.

Tribal groups have a hard life and are at the bottom of the social ladder, so to speak. Few people living near the reservations had compassion for or inclination to help those less fortunate. Some of the Kaingang lived on the outskirts of their towns and cities, but most of them were on reservations. It was not uncommon to hear, "The Kaingang and other people like them are lazy drunkards! It would be better if they were all dead."

We realized it was going to be very challenging, both for the Kaingang and the missionaries, to achieve a relationship that would make evangelism possible. Because of the treatment they had received from the townspeople, they'd find it difficult to trust us. And should we gain the trust of the Kaingang, there would be many layers of things for them to unlearn due to Catholicism's influence, to understand salvation by grace, and grace alone. And before they could feed themselves upon God's Word, they needed to learn to read, a skill, that up till now, they had felt no need to acquire. They would need a translation of the Scriptures in their own language, which was no longer pure, but so mixed with Portuguese that they could not have told you which were their own words, and which were taken from the language spoken around them by the townspeople. But to get back to the survey.

The first reservation we visited was referred to as either the Xanxere or Xapecó Reservation. (For the most part, reservations were named for the towns or cities they were near.)

We started out on March 16th with limited funds, so we determined to travel as economically as possible, meaning one meal a day, which was usually supper, and the cheapest form of transportation. We boarded a wood-burning train, riding second class, which took us to Porto Uniao, a town that bordered two states, Paraná and Santa Catarina: few places can claim that kind of distinction. From Porto Uniao we took a bus to the town of Xanxere.

Carrying our bags, we got off the bus at the junction of the road that would take us to the Reservation Headquarters about six kilometers away. We walked.

We arrived at the Reservation Headquarters on the 17th. Senhor Nereu, the post director, wasn't there, but his assistant welcomed us. We met the post director and his wife, Dona Lourdes, later. When we finally met him, we soon surmised he was an outspoken, political leftist and an agnostic. We noticed a Bible on his desk and were hopeful, but soon learned he kept it on hand so he could argue against it with more authority! (I haven't seen him for many years, but it was rumored that he eventually stopped arguing and became a believer!)

When we explained the reason for our visit to the reservation, despite his reputation, he was not antagonistic and even offered to put us up for the night. He told us that it was a large reservation: over a thousand Kaingang and Guarani in residence. He was very willing to have us help them in any way we could should we decide to start a work there.

The next reservation we planned to visit was the Guarita Indian Post in the state of Rio Grande do Sul.

To reach it involved a lot of bus travel! We went first to the city of Xapecó in the state of Santa Catarina, where we transferred to another bus bound for Nonoai, in the state of Rio Grande do Sul. While waiting for the bus that would take us on to Irai, one of several towns on the way to Guarita, we walked around Nonoai, a dismally hot town with dusty dirt roads. I looked at Floyd, shook my head, and said, "This place is the end of the world, I'd never want to live here!" I knew that there was a reservation near Nonoai, but was glad to be by-passing that one, looking more optimistically toward seeing what it was like at the Guarita Indian Post, 100 miles from this no-mans-land! (Never realizing I would one day be eating my words! God had planned for Ebba and me to work on the Nonoai Reservation for 17 years!)

Shortly after noon, the bus to Irai came, and with others, we climbed on, paid our fare, and decided to over-night at a hotel in Irai. The road was not very good, and the bus was constantly stopping to let someone off or to pick up others. At one stop, a blind man felt his way up the steps of the bus and sat down upon them when the driver closed the door. He was obviously a frequent traveler and a favorite of other passengers. He began to play his accordion and sang country folk songs as the bus bounced over rocks and ruts! We relaxed. It was quite entertaining.

In the morning, refreshed from a good night's sleep in Irai, we left on the last lap of our journey, headed for the Guarita Indian Post.

During the whole survey trip, we were given a good reception at every reservation we visited, which included being offered places to sleep, and whatever else we needed or wanted. The Guarita Post Director, Senhor Alísio de Carvalho, was no exception. He welcomed us, and we knew that were we to work on his post, we would have his cooperation. One of the most important objectives for the survey trip was to determine how those in charge of the reservations would accept us and our efforts to evangelize the Kaingang people. There were more than twenty reservations spread over three southern states, but we only had time to visit a few. Because the reservations consisted of both Kaingang and Guarani, we would concentrate on the Kaingang, but were certainly not blind to the needs of the Guarani people and would do all we could to reach them with the gospel as well. It was a mystery to us how these two ethnic groups had so much in common living on the reservations together but had managed to retain their own languages and customs!

The next reservation we planned to visit was the Ligeiro Indian Post. This post was not far from the small city of Getulio Vargas, in the state of Rio Grande do Sul. This post was by far the best organized and well-run we had seen. Floyd and I had a good talk with the Post Director, who shared so much with us that helped us to know how he managed things so efficiently. After that brief encounter and a good night's rest, the next morning, we took off again.

Next came the Cacique Doble Reservation, which was not far from the Uruguay River, which bordered the states of Rio Grande do Sul and Santa Catarina.

Arriving at the small city of Cacique Doble, we checked into a small hotel with board and room facilities where we could leave our bags before taking a taxi out to the reservation, four miles from town. It was evening when we arrived. Our visit there was short but cordial, and we were given supper before we walked back into the small city of Cacique Doble. It had been a long day, and we were happy we had already checked into the hotel! We rejoiced a little too soon: while we were gone, someone had come into our dormitory-like room and helped himself to the blanket on my bed! It was a cold, chilly night as I tried to sleep with the one remaining sheet!

It was also a short night—because we were catching a ride on a truck early the next morning to a riverside town called Marcelino Ramos, where we would catch a train back to Ponta Grossa and our families. The truck was not going into Marcelino Ramos, however, and let us off some nine kilometers from the town. We were walking, and none of the few vehicles that passed offered us a ride. We covered the nine kilometers on foot. When we were in sight of the city, a truck loaded with cobblestones stopped, and the driver asked, "You want a ride?" Did we ever!

Next came a fifteen-hour train ride. We'd been frugal, but we still had a few coins in our pockets when we arrived back in Ponta Grossa. We were so happy to see our wives, and they, too, have us back with stories to tell, all the funny things that happened, as well as the many opportunities we had encountered to work among a gospel-needy people: the Kaingang!

Floyd had made his choice and told his wife, "Ida, I'm very sure that God is leading us to the Xapecó Reservation near the town of Xanxere."

I was still undecided, however. But, unbelievably, after my negative feelings about the dusty, dirty town of Nonoai, I nevertheless felt I needed to visit the Nonoai Reservation that we'd passed up to go to the Guarita Indian Post. A couple of months later, in May of 1953, I returned to Nonoai.

But first, Ebba and I had a wedding to attend: that of my good friend Jack Vaughn, who was marrying Joanne. Now, all five of us singles who'd ventured together over the ocean waters to land in Brazil were married!

Rus Garber, director of NTM, was still in Brazil helping to open works among tribal groups still needing missionaries to bring them the Gospel. When I shared with him my desire to find out more about the Kaingang on the Nonoai Reservation, he volunteered to go with me. This was going to be a quicker route than the one Floyd Gilbert and I took on our survey trip. We flew to the city of Erechim, in the state of Rio Grande do Sul. And from there, took the 65-mile journey to Nonoai by taxi.

The first thing we did after the taxi driver deposited us in Nonoai was find a place to spend the night. We located a small, wooden hotel operated by Senhor Alfonso Gaboardi. The next morning, we were taken by taxi to the reservation about five kilometers from town. The director of the reservation was not there, so we decided to visit some of the houses near the reservation headquarters. We were fortunate to come to the home of Gumercindo, the chief (*cacique*) of the Kaingang on that reservation.

As we visited with Gumercindo, I somehow understood God to say: 'Alton, this is the place for you!' In our hurried visits on the survey I made with Floyd, we'd met officials in charge of the reservations but had little or no contact with the people. I think God wanted me to experience interaction with a Kaingang person before he could make his will known to me. God had orchestrated things: the Director of the Nonoai Reservation was absent, and we 'happened upon' chief Gumercindo's house.

I shared how I felt with Russ, who was a great encourager and forward thinker. "Well, Alton, we'd better see what's available for housing in the town since you probably won't be allowed to live on the reservation," he said. Reluctantly, we left Gumercindo and the reservation, and talked about all the possibilities as we walked the five kilometers back into town.

Upon arrival, we began inquiring about housing, were directed to a general store, and told to talk to Senhor Edgar Winkler. I told Senhor Winkler that I was looking for a place to rent and would be returning in about a month to move in.

"I know just the place for you!" he said enthusiastically. "There's an old house right in the center of town, facing the plaza and handy to everything." The location seemed good: it was handy to stores, but he wasn't kidding about the house being old. When Senhor Edgar showed us the inside of the house, he said, "There are a few things that need done, but I'll have it all fixed up for you before you return in a month!" The "few things" included: fixing the leaks in the roof, replacing the broken windowpanes, painting the walls inside the house, etcetera, etcetera, etcetera!

Taking him at his word, I told him, "I'll take it."

It might have been good to pay more attention to his joyful disclosure concerning who our neighbors would be. "Two fine Roman Catholic priests are on one side of the house, and on the other side is a grade school operated by nuns!"

Later, when I tried to describe the house to Ebba, all I could think of to tell her was: "It's a brick house, and its walls are at least twelve inches thick!" And to myself, I said, "No need telling her the condition of the house: it'll be all fixed up when we move in."

That taken care of, Russ and I took the noon bus to the city of Passo Fundo, where we'd been told we could find Senhor Francisco, the director of the Nonoai Reservation. We slept in a hotel that night, and the next morning, we located the director at another hotel.

I told him that I had visited the reservation and was disappointed to learn he was away, and that I was told we could locate him in Passo Fundo. I introduced myself and Rus, explained to him that I would be moving to Nonoai, and was hoping to work with the Kaingang people at the reservation. He listened politely and showed a cooperative attitude, and put up no opposition to our working there. This was further indication of God's open door and His calling to Nonoai.

And so ended May with my heart settled on where God wanted Ebba and me to serve him as a married couple. This work would be so different from what I had experienced my first months in Brazil, first with Joel, and then with Jack: visiting and evangelizing in out-of-the-way places in central Brazil. I had Joel to orient and train me for that work, but I had no one who'd worked on reservations before me to clue me in. This time, I'd be on my own. But I had the right wife to help me, and the Lord, who promised never to leave me nor forsake me, and who, after all, had commanded us to go into all nations with his Gospel, no matter how different and needy the people, and that made it seem less daunting.

CHAPTER EIGHT

NONOAI

month before our first anniversary, Ebba and I set out for Nonoai, the dusty no-man's-land that I wanted *nothing* to do with the first time I landed there on the survey trip that I took with Floyd Gilbert. But God: it is amazing how he works in our hearts! I submitted to his will and ended up living in Nonoai for seventeen years. It certainly wasn't the ideal place to bring a new wife and to adjust to a new marriage, but Ebba and I both were ready for the sacrifices and hardships during ministry; we'd settled that long before in our Boot Camp training in Fouts Springs.

We flew from Ponta Grossa, where we had been living with the Gilberts, to Passo Fundo, in the state of Rio Grande do Sul. Some missionaries in that city, from another mission, very kindly invited us to stay with them for a few days so that we could make some last-minute purchases to set up housekeeping in Nonoai. Of all the things we purchased in Passo Fundo, the most important item was the wood cook stove . The south of Brazil can get very cold, and we were going to need the stove for more than just cooking.

On June 6, 1953, we said goodbye to our missionary friends in Passo Fundo, thanked them for their hospitality, and boarded a bus for

Nonoai, 90 miles away. We traveled over dirt roads, and it was a cold, rainy trip.

The things we'd sent by truck arrived ahead of us, and had been taken to the house I'd rented from Senhor Edgar Winkler, the storekeeper. That was the good news! The bad news? None of the promised repairs on the house had been done! We moved in anyway: there was no other choice. Fortunately, we had a well for water in the backyard. We could cook, wash, and drink!

There were two apartments in the old house, each with three rooms. Down a hallway from our apartment lived Dona Ambrosia, the mother of Senhor Edgar. For whatever reason unknown to me, the repairs on the house were never done. So, a little at a time, I did them myself. Dona Ambrosia was a frequent visitor, and Ebba learned more about Brazilian cooking from her. Often, in the evenings, she would come down the hall and into our part of the house to visit us. She was a sweet older lady and a devout Roman Catholic. In our evening visits, Ebba and I would explain salvation by faith in Christ.

Little by little, we worked on obtaining furnishings for the three rooms in our apartment. The mattress that was mentioned earlier on in our story was laid on the floor of the bedroom. For the first few days, we sat on crates and held our plates in our laps at mealtimes in the kitchen. When we first arrived, our living conditions could be accurately referred to as simple to the extreme! At night, I slept with a flashlight and my 22-caliber rifle beside me. It wasn't to protect us from burglars, unless you'd refer to huge rats by this designation! When I heard a rat running around, I'd shine the flashlight on it and shoot it. I didn't bother to get up to remove the rat or rats until morning came.

A local carpenter agreed to make us a table, and we set out to look for chairs. That took a while, but we finally found some. We also found a bed for the mattress and felt we'd really come up in the world: literally! I made a few cupboards and shelves, we learned where to shop for food, and soon, living conditions, though still simple, were much better.

Then came the suspicions and oppositions! From the start, the townspeople were curious, wondering what we were doing in Nonoai where no other foreigners lived. But as soon as the priests perceived that we were Protestants, word was out, and people began to avoid us. We had heard that the town had prided itself on not having permitted Protestants to live there. They began to put pressure on Dona Ambrosia to get us out of her house. Schoolchildren were told that if they had anything to do with us, they would be expelled from school.

Over the years we lived in Nonoai, occasionally someone would come to our door for a visit. After talking about the weather, the crops in the fields, and other things, they would get to the real reason for their visit. They wanted my help to locate buried treasures, boxes, and trunks full of gold, silver, and precious stones: dating from the time when the Jesuit priests had been expelled from Brazil, well over a hundred years before. If I would help them find these treasures, we could divide them, and both be rich! These covetous people were convinced I had some device for detecting buried metals, and stood a good chance of unearthing them.

Rest assured, I let them know that I was there to tell them about a different kind of treasure!

The first few months we lived in Nonoai were not easy. Aside from the mistrust a few of the people had for us, a couple of tragedies took place that were quite unsettling. A neighbor of ours, the wife of a shoemaker, for some unknown reason, poisoned the well from which they got their water and killed several members of her family. After that, there was a gun battle between two local policemen and some trespassing hunters:

the policemen got the worst of the fight. A true wild west atmosphere prevailed in Nonoai, especially on weekends, when people were drinking.

Several days a week, I would walk to and from the reservation, and this left Ebba alone from early morning till nearly dark. It was a five-kilometer hike, and that was just to get to the Reservation Headquarters. The Kaingang did not have a central village, but lived scattered all over the huge reservation; there was no way to gather a large group for meetings at first.

During the winter season, June, July, and August, a very heavy fog hangs over the area until nine or ten o'clock in the morning; despite this, I would leave home early to make trips to *Kaingang-land.* On other days, it would be too foggy to attempt it, and Ebba and I would work around our house and yard. I made additional cupboards, fixed windows, cleaned up junk left in the yard by previous renters, and prepared as much as possible for the birth of our first child, due in September.

The permit that we'd been granted did not allow us to overnight on the reservation, and that is why we needed to live in Nonoai, and travel between town and the reservation to begin a ministry among the Kaingang. On nice days, I walked a minimum of 11 or 12 miles, and on many days as many as 20 to visit as many homes as I could. Making friends with these isolated people and gaining their confidence took a long time. They were rightfully suspicious of me. After all, what American in his right mind would be walking all those miles just to preach to them for a few hours! As they tried to figure me out, they were sure I must have a secondary motive. (I later learned this was the feeling of the townspeople, as well: *What does that white man want with the Kaingang and those of us in the village? He's up to something!)*

But I was persistent and continued my visits. I'd approach a house, clap my hands, and call out, "Hello, Good Morning!" If the man of the house were present, he'd show himself. But if not, the women and children would either lock themselves in their houses, or if they saw me coming, would be hiding out in the nearby woods. And for a long time, nothing changed!

CHAPTER NINE

A LITTLE CHILD SHALL LEAD THEM

We began taking trips to Passo Fundo, a couple hours' drive from Nonoai, to see a Christian Doctor there who would deliver our baby at the end of September 1953. Ebba had some health problems relative to the pregnancy, and on one of these trips, Dr. Ademar Petracco recommended we stay in Passo Fundo for the last three weeks of the pregnancy.

We rented a room in the Hotel Franz, which was in the center of town. Of course, at that time, no one knew what the baby would be, so we kept discussing names: boys names and girls names! We also had time to gather the baby clothes and other things we would soon be needing.

While waiting for our baby, the Lord brought Jack Vaughn back into our lives, and with him, his new wife Joanne! They'd only been married four months, and this would be their first ministry together. They arrived in Passo Fundo on the afternoon of September 28th.

Jack and I had lots of conversations about the Kaingang, and approaches to ministry. Because we had to live in Nonoai and travel quite a distance to get to the reservation, and because of how vast the reservation was, we were going to need to purchase bicycles. I took Jack to the same store where I'd bought mine, and he purchased one just like it. I was really looking forward to working with Jack again, and Ebba was thrilled to have another woman to fellowship with.

Ebba went into labor, and we hurried to the hospital. The birth progressed normally, and I was allowed to attend the event! When Arlene Gail Cothron was washed, dressed in some of the pretty clothes, and wrapped in the little blankets Ebba had brought to the hospital, they handed her to *me* to carry to Ebba's room. I'll always remember walking down the hospital hall, carrying *my baby* carefully as though she were glass and might break. It was a strange, new feeling to hold our child and to be called a father!

Dr. Petracco was concerned about Ebba being so thin. Before sending us home, he prescribed a good supply of vitamins and other things to build her up and give her an appetite. We returned to Nonoai on October 12, 1953.

Bringing a tiny little baby into town with us seemed to open the hearts of the townspeople: they seemed to ignore the prohibitions of the priests and nuns in their eagerness to see our new baby. They came into our house and exclaimed over Arlene with smiles and happiness! And even her colic and crying brought out their sympathy, suggestions, and compassion! Truly, *a little child shall lead them!*

Dona Ambrosia had moved out, so Jack and Joanne moved into the apartment down the hall from us.

Music is another thing that breaks down barriers. Joanne played the accordion very well and this attracted a lot of attention right away and gave opportunities to witness and shine the light of Christ in a community that had been in darkness for so long. Soon, we held preaching services in our home or in other homes that opened to us.

When the weather was good, Jack and I would bid our wives goodbye, hop on our bikes, and take off for the reservation. Because some of the Kaingang knew Portuguese quite well, we could explain salvation to them right away, but we wanted to learn their language, and understand their culture and customs for all those who didn't speak Portuguese.

Gumercindo, the Kaingang chief, was also known by the title of *Coronel*. We visited Coronel often in his house, which was located on the main road in front of the Post Headquarters. Soon, we became very good friends. He spoke and understood Portuguese quite well, and was a good person on which to share the message of salvation. He was drinking in God's Word like a sponge! I'm hopeful that he died a believer. There will be more about my good friend Gumercindo later in the story.

One day, Jack and I were heading out to the reservation. About a mile out of town, we met a man coming into town with a wagon pulled by two horses. Jack and I took our bikes off the road to avoid scaring the horses, but too late! The horses spooked, jumped over a bank with the wagon, resulting in the tongue of the wagon breaking. Naturally, the man was upset. We heard him out, and then I gave him a note to take to Ebba, authorizing her to give him money for a new tongue for the wagon.

Wouldn't you know, we met this same man in the late afternoon as we were returning home? This time, however, we took our bicycles *way off the road* and hid them in the tall grass until the wagon and team of horses were past us.

Ebba and I lived in Nonoai for seventeen years. A day-by-day account of our time there is hardly possible and would no doubt be redundant in many ways, so I will limit myself to some of the main events that occurred during those years.

We lived for one year in the old house on the town square with the Vaughns, who, after a year and a half, left Nonoai to work in another area.

We soon realized we needed a place of our own. We didn't go looking for one, but when a whole city block on the east side of town came up for sale, we decided to buy it. People were moving out of Nonoai to places that were more prosperous, and were selling their homes and properties for a good price. There were two frame houses and a rickety barn on the property we purchased.

I tore down one of the houses that was beyond repair and used that lumber to fix up the other house, which became quite livable after doing the needed repairs. The barn served as it was for quite a while, but later, I tore it down and built a new one a few feet from where the original barn had been. There was a good-sized garden, planted and producing mandioca (yuca root) and squash. These were the vegetables we depended on the most, and this garden greatly helped our financial situation.

Once settled into the renovated house, we began making plans to build ourselves a new house right in the middle of our property, a much better place for a residence.

I had been a watch repairman before going to Brazil but knew nothing about building. My friend Floyd Gilbert, on the other hand, had lots of experience in construction. He volunteered to come from Xanxere to help me get started. He couldn't take too much time away from his own work, so he helped me with the plans, and left instructions on how to proceed when he returned to Xanxere.

To make the foundation for our house, I hired a man with a truck, and we went out of town a few miles on the road to the city of Erechim and brought back rocks, some of them quite large. I mixed the cement by hand and laid the rocks up until I had a foundation almost two and a half feet high on the backside of the house. The house was small, only twenty feet by thirty feet. Unlike most of the houses in Nonoai, our new house had horizontal wood siding and, not as common, windows with glass. After painting the siding with oil-based paint, it looked very nice. There were two bedrooms, a small washroom meant to be a bathroom someday, and a combination living, dining room, and kitchen. Our toilet was old fashioned, an outside privy. A few years later, we added another bedroom and a separate kitchen with a good-sized pantry. With the additions and a new garage, our living conditions were more modern, and housekeeping much easier.

For the first six years, our water supply was a spring that was located about seventy-five yards down the hill behind our house. We carried water up in five-gallon kerosene cans. When electricity became available, I built a small pump-house, installed a pump, and piped water up to the house. This system served us for the rest of the years we lived in Nonoai.

We had a good-sized pasture and decided to buy a Holstein cow when it came up for sale. I had never milked a cow before, and this cow had never been milked before! But, with a combination of practice on my part, and patience on the cow's, we both adjusted to each other quite well. From that time on, we were well-supplied with milk and butter.

Our Holstein cow later had a calf, which we named *Surprise!* One morning, we went out to the barn, and unexpectedly, there stood a calf beside our milk cow, so we all agreed that *Surprise* would be its name! Besides milk and butter, our cow supplied us with many other surprises and laughs in the succeeding years! She was a regular escape artist! No fence could keep her in the pasture if she wanted out, and no matter where we tied her, she found a way to get loose! Ebba stayed away from the pasture, convinced that our cow did not like women, and if she did go into the pasture, she soon hurried out when the cow started after her!

However, our second daughter, Beatriz, had a way with all animals and, at age eight, began milking our cow. I stayed nearby, of course, at first, but she did a good job of it, and both Beatriz and the cow seemed to enjoy themselves immensely whenever milking time came around.

Grapes were very plentiful in southern Brazil, partly due to the Italian immigrant population. Ebba and I learned how to make grape juice, and each year around the month of January, we spent several days making grape juice, which we stored in a little cellar under the pantry off the kitchen.

Arlene, from the time she was a baby, liked to ride horses. I remember going down to the water-powered gristmill, about a half mile from our house, on horseback with Arlene sitting on the saddle in front of me. When I dismounted to open the gate, holding tightly to the reins and keeping one eye on Arlene, I'd lead her through the gate, alone on the horse, as I opened and shut it! She'd hold tightly to the horn of the saddle and look so important!

Arlene was such a darling little child! We'd take her with us to meetings, and she loved playing *preacher!* She would go around the house picking up the Bible and saying verses we had taught her. We called her our little missionary, because she would tell people who would come to our house that they needed to accept Jesus to go to heaven. From a little girl on, Arlene liked to help with the work. She had a little red wagon in which she would load sticks and take them to the barn where we stored the firewood.

A middle-aged neighbor lady named Dona Otilia was our wash lady. One day, when we were at her house picking up laundry, Dona Otilia didn't look too tidy, having worked hard all day. Arlene noticed! She looked at her and said, "Dona Otilia, please comb your hair and put a ribbon in it," for all the world sounding like Ebba when she was correcting Arlene. Another time, Arlene inspected the condition of the vertical slats in the walls of Dona Otilia's house that had dried over time and separated, letting in the daylight. This time, she said, "Dona Otilia, your house is all ripped."

Kids will do and say such cute things. We should have recorded all the things our kids said that made us laugh, but alas, we didn't. Here is one example, however. When our son Derly was still a toddler, I was lying on the ground under our Jeep lubricating the various parts with a manual grease gun. Derly asked me, "What is that thing?" I told him it was a grease gun. Derly, looking a little startled, said, "Daddy, are you going to kill the Jeep?" We had a good laugh over that one, too!

I'm sure that having a normal family life, complete with children, helped greatly to bring about an end to the distrust and disapproval we met with when we first moved into Nonoai. The townspeople became more receptive to us, and to God's Word, because of our children, who could speak Portuguese like natives from the start, and interacted with the people, as one of them! Yes, I'm convinced, *even a little child will lead them.*

CHAPTER TEN

VEHICLES AND VICTROLAS

*T*wo things prompted us to leave the three-room apartment where we'd been living for a year on the town square: we knew that the work God had set before us was going to take time and that we wouldn't be moving out of Nonoai in the very near future, and the fact that our little family was growing! Three small rooms were not going to be enough!

When we moved from our tiny apartment and settled into our temporary house, I resumed my trips to the Kaingang Reservation by bike. The bicycle was fine where the roads or trails were good, but sometimes, weather conditions made it almost impossible to travel about the reservation on a bike.

Now that we were on our own property and had a barn and a pasture, I decided to buy a horse and a saddle. I had experienced traveling by horse during the months I worked in the interior of the country, but didn't really have that much experience picking one out. I took my time, trying to select the right one for me. The horse I picked seemed very tame, was reddish in color, and had a nice, relaxed, marching gait.

In Brazil, people say there are only two kinds of horsemen: those who have fallen off their horses and those that *would soon* fall off! Well said! I fulfill both categories!

One day, I mounted my *very tame, reddish colored horse, with a relaxed, marching gait,* and headed out to the Kaingang Reservation. The day went well on the reservation, but on my way I had to go up and down some hills. I was riding along nicely, going down a long, steep hill when my horse suddenly stumbled and I was thrown over its head, and landed about ten feet down the hill. The horse, rolled downhill as well, but regained its feet before I did mine, and stood there looking at me. I was not hurt except for my pride! I looked both ways to make sure no one had seen me fall, brushed myself off, and walked up to get back on my horse. I slowly extended my hand to grab the reins, but he wasn't going to have any of it! He turned away and walked a few steps up the hill, stopped, and looked back at me as though saying, *can I trust you?* This happened several times, and I began to wonder if I would end up walking all the way into town led by a horse dragging its reins! It took a while, but eventually, I mounted my *very tame horse,* which carried me the rest of the way home without incident!

I kept progressing from one manner of travel to another: from walking, to biking, from biking to horseback, and from horseback to a motor vehicle!

I traveled to Campinas, São Paulo for mission meetings in late April of 1955. While there, I bought a 1947 Studebaker station wagon; the original motor had been replaced with a 1948 Chevrolet motor. We used this vehicle for about five years. Feeling no need now for the bicycle or the horse, I sold them, but soon regretted getting rid of my bike! It would have helped for little trips around town, such as to the post office.

The Kaingang were enchanted with riding in the station wagon! Many times, as I drove into the reservation, someone would come running out of his house, flag me down, and ask for a ride. My question usually was, "Where are you going?" The answer was always, "Nowhere."

They didn't lack the courage to ride in the car. It was a thrill for them! When I'd stop to pick up the one flagging me down, others would come running, and as many as could get in, did! I worried about overloading the car. They had little or no concept of weight, and if there was room to squeeze more people in, they did.

On one occasion, I had to insist that some of them get out of the car before I would continue the trip. When no one budged, I got out. I sat down beside the road and told them, "I am going nowhere until some of you get out."

I gave the number of how many that should be, and after arguing among themselves for a while, that was the number that reluctantly climbed out! I got back into the car, started it up, and we drove off, still overloaded!

The ministry on the reservation was so much easier now that I had a vehicle, even though sometimes it was a distraction!

Gradually, we gained the trust of the people in Nonoai. They would visit us, and we them. We began to make friends. During the day, I worked on the reservation, but on evenings and weekends, we visited our friends and others. Even though the priests had told the people to have nothing to do with us, we were soon accepted wherever we went.

One Sunday, our former landlord, Senhor Edgar Winkler, and his wife, came to the house and invited us to go with them to visit his brother and family, who lived on a farm a few miles out of town. We took our wind-up Victrola with us, and some of the records produced by Gospel Recordings. Out of curiosity, if nothing else, they listened to the gospel messages, and to the hymns we played for them.

While still traveling by bicycle, I would tie the Victrola on the back of the bike when I visited the Kaingang Reservation. The first few times when I wound up the Victrola and put a record on to play, the people would be amazed to hear voices coming from a "box" with no one around. They would circle around and around the Victrola, talking among themselves and laughing about it! The big question in their minds was: *how can a man fit inside that little box?*

At that time, I did not have records in the Kaingang language to play, only in Portuguese: but it didn't seem to matter whether they understood the voice that was speaking, they'd still come to hear the man in the box. Later, however, I taped Bible lessons in the Kaingang language on a tape recorder. These were well received and drew people who did want to hear what was being said!

It's amazing how just living in a place, just being present, is used by the Lord. Even in everyday dealings, and circumstances, God uses our lives. Before having our own cow, we had been buying milk from a lady in town who sold milk. Her nine or ten-year-old son Batista would come to our house on horseback each morning to bring us milk. When he'd leave the milk in the kitchen, Ebba would talk to him about Jesus and salvation. She set up the flannelgraph board in our living room, and would invite Batista to stay a few minutes to hear a Bible story she illustrated with flannel-backed figures. We believe Batista was the first person to be saved in the village of Nonoai because he delivered milk to a kind lady who took an interest in him.

Ebba was able to lead a schoolteacher, by the name of Geni, to the Lord, because of friendly conversations with her, and showing appreciation for her teaching our daughters, Arlene and Beatriz, in the small grade school in Nonoai.

Other opportunities like these came about or were given to us by the Lord in answer to our prayers. The Gospel was there waiting to be shared, lost souls unknowingly awaited the day they would know God, and the Holy Spirit orchestrated our contacts with them.

CHAPTER ELEVEN

THE PROS, AND CONS, UPS, AND DOWNS OF MINISTRY

Soon after we moved to Nonoai in mid-1953, I began walking out to the Kaingang Reservation.

I ran into someone who told me about a man named Pedro Marcos who lived on the reservation even though he was not a Kaingang. He was one of many Brazilians who leased parcels of farmland and paid a percentage of the harvest to the Kaingang Post Headquarters.

Pedro Marcos must have been in his seventies when I first met him. He was always jolly and easy to visit with. But on my first visit, things didn't go too well. I started to tell him about the meaning of Christ's death on the cross, that it was to pay the debt we owed for our sins, and that this would make us right with God. Pedro stopped me mid-explanation, and told me, "I was born a Roman Catholic and I will die a Roman Catholic. How about you keep your religion to yourself, and I'll keep mine to myself. Then, we can be good friends." He went on to tell me, "Anytime you are on the reservation and need a place to stay, you're welcome to come to our house; just don't talk about religion."

"Wouldn't you like to read about it, at least?" I asked smiling, handing him a tract. He wouldn't take it, but to show that he wasn't upset, when I was about to leave, he gave me a sweet potato to take home to my wife: a huge one! I thanked him, but dreaded having to carry it on my twelve-kilometer hike back to Nonoai. Had it not been for my tender conscience, I would have thrown it in the bushes! Pedro got around to asking me later, "Did your family enjoy the sweet potato I sent home with you?" And I could honestly say that they did!

I stopped by his house occasionally, and developed a good friendship with him and his wife. Pedro had a lot of beehives in the woods near his home, and one day, offered to give me a swarm. "You make the box, and I'll teach you how to work with bees," he offered.

And when my box was built, Pedro was as good as his word. He was a good teacher, and I really enjoyed working with bees. He didn't have all the modern paraphernalia for extracting honey, but taught me to use a smoking rag to make the bees leave the hive when I cut the honeycomb from the forms and put them in big cans or basins. Bees were all around me while I was doing this, but I learned that they don't usually sting unless they sense you fear them, or you injure a bee in some of the handling. We had all the honey we needed and more. On visits to the Bible Institute, or to mission headquarters, I would take honey to other missionaries.

As part of their missions course at the Bible Institute, students were sent to help missionaries in their fields of service to gain experience. We enjoyed those who came to observe our work with the Kaingang. One of those students, Sergio, accompanied me out to visit my friend Pedro Marcos when I heard that he was sick. We took our instruments on that visit, my violin and Sergio's trombone. By this time, the Lord had softened Pedro's heart to the point that he didn't refuse us when we asked if he would like us to play and sing hymns. And before we left, he even let us pray with him. From that time on, the door was open to teach him and his wife from the Bible, and they allowed us to hold services in their house. We were able to reach other members of their family with the gospel, as well. Pedro's health went from bad to worse, and he finally died. Even though I am not sure of his salvation, I'm so grateful for the many good opportunities he had to hear the gospel, and for the assurance of God's Word that says: *"So shall my word be that goes forth out of my mouth: it shall not return unto me void, but it shall accomplish that which I please, and it shall prosper in the thing whereto I sent it."* (Isaiah 55:11)

While Sergio was with us, we began taking our instruments all over the Kaingang Reservation, and into the homes of many Brazilians in or around the reservation. We'd play and sing duets, and our music was quite an attraction, not because we were professional musicians, but in the interior of the country, any music was a treat. After having played and sung some hymns, we would generally preach a clear gospel message. God used our efforts, and Sergio and I enjoyed performing together for God's Glory!

The more we ministered in Nonoai, the more we came to expect the unexpected; sometimes we tended to wonder if any real fruit would come from our efforts, but we plodded along, taking advantage of every opportunity to plant seed. We had to water some of that seed for many years before we saw hearts soften, but since the Holy Spirit was our leader and facilitator, pleasing Him was more important to us than seeing results. We trusted Him to give the increase in his own time and to use the opportunities, trials, and experiences that were ours along the way!

One thing I could depend on, I thought, was my sturdy good health! Other than occasional colds and flu, I was never very sick during the first few years in Brazil, and really, for the rest of the 47 years we were in that country. But in 1955, I realized I did have feet of clay!

Somewhere and somehow, I had been exposed to a dreaded disease before the day we entertained a Brazilian believer who had come to visit us from his farm quite a distance from Nonoai. He'd travelled on horseback, and it was evident that both he and his horse needed a good rest, and we urged him to do so: *in our house*! We had a good visit and by the time he left I was feeling bad.

We waved goodbye, and watched him trot out of sight! When we went back into the house, I finally gave in to how poorly I had been feeling for a while. I told Ebba, "You know what, I have a terrible headache; I think I'd better lie down." She took my temperature, and sure enough, I had a high fever. I perspired so much that I soaked my bed. After three days in bed with no improvement, we thought I'd better be seen by a doctor.

The nearest medical facility was in the city of Xapecó, which was in the state of Santa Catarina. We finally asked a friend in town if he would drive us there, since I knew that I wouldn't be able to drive that far in my condition. Arriving at the hospital, I was seen by a doctor who quickly diagnosed my illness as *typhoid fever*. After being treated in the hospital for three days, and after my constant claims to be much better, the doctor released me to return home, warning, "But you must agree to rest and take certain precautions, or you will end up back in the hospital!"

Ebba didn't think it wise to take me home so soon, but I was determined. I also decided I could drive back to Nonoai. When we got home, Ebba kept watch over me, fed me Brazilian-style chicken soup, and before long, I was as good as new, eager to pick up my ministries with the Kaingang again!

We had become friends with a young, newly married couple while they were living in one of the houses on our property. The man was called by a nickname which was Polaco (Polish) and his wife was Jura. They were not believers, and we were hoping to lead them to the Lord. One day Polaco came over and asked to borrow a knife. Not suspecting trouble, I loaned it to him.

A few days later, he went to a Saturday night dance where he had an altercation with another man, who also had a knife! Polaco had taken my knife with him, but the other man stabbed him first.

The excitement began in the middle of the night, and it was dark and pouring down rain when someone knocked on our door. I answered and was told, "Polaco is wounded, and we are looking for someone to take him to Ronda Alta to see the doctor there!"

I agreed to take him, although it was thirty miles away and it was raining very hard, and the road up the hill to the main street was very muddy! I tried, but found traction on the long driveway impossible! I finally gave up and went to the home of a man who had a jeep. After much persuasion and my promise to pay for the trip, he agreed to make the trip. It took us three hours as we plowed through mud and water! At one point, Polaco asked us to stop so he could get out and relieve himself. Standing in the downpour of rain, he fainted in my arms. We finally arrived in Ronda Alta and the doctor on duty at the small hospital told me, "I'll operate, but there's little hope that your friend Polaco will live through the surgery." To everyone's surprise, he did.

Later, after returning home, I told him, "Polaco, you need the Lord!" He made a profession of faith, but his life didn't change.

We could tell that Jura really had a difficult time living with her husband, and we hoped that, somehow, they would come to know the Lord and that their marriage would heal.

Floyd Gilbert, who was working with the Kaingang in Xanxere, needed a man to work for him on his farm. He invited Polaco and Jura to come home with him. Unfortunately, it didn't work out: Polaco didn't like farm work, and they soon left Xanxere. We lost track of them, though we kept praying that the Lord would bring them to Himself.

More excitement! Again, it was in the middle of the dark night, when we awoke to the sound of gunshots, not really knowing where they'd come from. We looked out the window, and the sky was illuminated, and we could see that a house was on fire. I dressed quickly and ran toward the fire with others to attempt to put it out. The gunshots were used to signal that there was a fire.

As with all the houses in Nonoai, this one was built with wooden walls and shingles, and it didn't have much of a chance of surviving! An elderly couple of Italian descent with whom we'd become quite friendly lived there. Simon, the husband, a carpenter, had done some work for us soon after we moved to Nonoai, and I had repaired an old mantle clock for him. We had told them of our faith in Jesus, and that Jesus could save them. They'd listened politely, but remained very strong Catholics.

Our little town did not have a fire department, but we formed a bucket brigade, drawing water from a well to fight the fire. We managed to save two neighboring houses, but unfortunately, Simon's house and possessions were a total loss. A man, drunk enough to enter the burning house without fear, managed to save two items from their house: a sewing machine and a mattress, as I recall! I felt so sorry for Senhor Simon and his wife.

Though our main ministry was with the Kaingang, as residents of Nonoai, whatever concerned the people living there, became our concerns as well!

In June of 1956 there was more excitement! The Kaingang people were staging a protest over the transfer of the Indian Post Inspector,

Senhor Francisco. He had been Post Inspector for close to fifteen years and the people did not want him to leave. Furthermore, they disliked the person who was designated to take his place. They armed themselves with guns and bows and arrows, and blocked all the roads in and out of the reservation. Several hundred of them left the reservation, and marched into town to stage a protest with the Justice of the Peace.

The regional inspector of the Indian Protective Service was called in to settle the dispute along with Senhor Nereu Costa, the director of the Xanxere Indian Post where Floyd and Ida Gilbert worked. These men came to see me and asked if I would help put down the demonstration, since I was the only one the Kaingang would let set foot on their land. I went along with them to help with the mediation. After much discussion and dialogue, a peaceful arrangement was found. Senhor Nereu was grateful, and, although an atheist, gave us missionaries much liberty to visit his Post in Santa Catarina.

In anticipation of our second baby's birth, I traveled to Xapecó to withdraw money from the bank where our monthly allowances were sent. Much to my surprise, I was informed, "There are no funds in your account."

The bank had not received proper communication from the sending bank in São Paulo, and until they did, we could not withdraw money. This meant we would not be able to pay for the hospital in Passo Fundo when the baby was born, nor could we afford a hotel while there.

"Money or not," I told myself, "That baby will soon make its appearance!"

So, soon after I returned home, we got things ready and took off for Passo Fundo. Once again, God had everything in control. Arriving in Passo Fundo, some missionary friends from another mission asked us to stay in their house while they were away attending to some medical issues of their own. And we accepted gratefully!

On July 16, 1956, Beatriz Claudette Cothron was born with no complications! Before long, the bank situation was fixed, the hospital was paid, and we returned to Nonoai, the proud parents of two little girls. Beatriz didn't have colic for which we were very happy, remembering the constant crying of Arlene who had suffered with it for several months.

Arlene and Beatriz brought much joy to our home: Arlene was our little *preacher/communicator,* and Beatriz was a *lover of animals* - dogs, cats, and especially cows. And both girls loved horses. Before long, we saw that Beatriz had a *tomboy-side*: she loved to climb trees and play soccer with the neighborhood boys even though that was not considered lady like!

That same year, 1956, near the small town of Jacutinga, in the state of Minas Gerais, the '*Instituto Evangélico Missionário*' was founded by Paul Guiley, a recent arrival to Brazil. The name was later changed to '*Instituto Bíblico Peniel.*'

By 1957, a requirement for completing missionary training at the Institute was to work for up to six months with missionaries who had established ministries. The system had some merit, but also some problems. In general, it was a good arrangement.

Ebba and I helped to train students from the Bible Missionary Institute, who came to work with us. The first to arrive was a young man by the name of Alberto. When the time came for our first furlough in 1958, he and another student, Sergio, lived in our home, used our vehicle, and carried on the work with the Kaingang and in the village of Nonoai in our absence. A short time later, they were joined by a married couple with small children.

When we returned from furlough in early 1959, Alberto had already gone back to the Institute. Soon after we arrived, Sergio and the married couple, Armando and Julieta, also returned to resume their studies.

From the very first, our sending church in Englewood, Colorado, gave sacrificially to our work in Brazil. Some of that had to do, of course, with the support we received monthly, but it went far beyond that to help with ministry needs, such as the various vehicles that facilitated our travels! With the funds the members of this church collected in 1959, we were able to buy a new Willys Jeep. The old Studebaker was sold to another missionary who needed it for his ministry.

The roads on which we traveled were hard on motor vehicles of any category, and that is why we appreciated the fact that the new Jeep had a metal cab that could take quite a beating as we drove to and from, and on, the Kaingang Reservation in all kinds of weather. The standard equipment for our vehicle, besides being four-wheel drive, was a machete, a 21-foot tow cable, chains for the wheels, a small folding shovel, some rope, a small axe or hatchet. Even with all this, there were a few times I had to go looking for someone with a team of oxen to get my vehicle out of a mudhole.

The Jeep was, however, small for our family, and after some time, we upgraded to a Jeep Station Wagon. It was a four-wheel-drive vehicle, definitely a big help in getting us to all the places we regularly visited: witnessing, holding services, and teaching literacy classes.

Most of the roads on the reservation were old, abandoned, logging roads that were not maintained by anyone. It didn't take long for each new vehicle to show its vulnerability to the treatment we were forced to put it through.

Whatever we felt would be useful in ministry, if they heard about it, either the church or an individual in our sending church would provide it! Take, for instance, the slide projector and the loudspeaker system that could be operated from the batteries in our vehicles. These were provided by the church in Englewood, Colorado, and were items we used for years in our ministry among the Kaingang.

We used the slide projector and loudspeaker system like this: I would drive into the reservation in the morning, and before starting my visits, I would find someone who would give me permission to return in the evening and hold a service in their yard. The rest of the day was spent visiting neighbors and inviting them to come in the evening to listen to the hymns being played over the sound system and to see the slides on the life of Christ, or Old Testament stories.

At first, I would pin a white sheet on the outside wall of the house on which to show slides, and later upgraded to a large screen. I would often show a few slides of their own people first! This generated interest and it was fun to see the Kaingang crowd about the screen, laughing and commenting about someone's face, his big nose, or funny expression. I always had Portuguese Bibles to sell and tracts to give out to those who could read. Nights with a full moon were especially good for this type of ministry because the audience, Kaingang and Brazilian, could see to walk to and from their homes. Anywhere from twenty-five to seventy-five people would attend. A lot of people were reached with the Gospel in this way, and the results came in unexpected ways, sometimes much later.

Many years had gone by when Ebba and I met a Brazilian lady who told us, "I remember how proud the families were who let you have meetings in their yards. I accepted Christ as a child at one of those meetings!"

Our sending church also provided Ebba with another important ministry tool that she used, not only with children, but also with the women she ministered to in the village of Nonoai: a complete set of Old and New Testament Flannelgraph lessons. Not only did Ebba make good use of this material with groups of people in the town, but it even made its way into the public school in Nonoai! One of the ladies she had taught through the series worked at the local school, and that lady was invited to teach Bible stories, using the flannelgraph figures, in the class on Religion.

Not everyone approved of our evangelism efforts, however! We continued to have active opposition, and came to expect it. Senhor Evilazio and his Christian family were eager for us to evangelize where they lived, beside the Passo Fundo River. The problem was the road! It was not a road for vehicles at all, but existed for ox carts. When I told Evilazio that I didn't think my vehicle could make it down the steep, narrow, rocky road, he said, "We'll work on that!"

Evilazio measured the width of our Jeep and proceeded to widen the existing oxcart road with his team of oxen and a plow. He asked for my help when he needed it, as when he had to blast some huge rocks in one spot, using dynamite, to make the road more passable. Even with these improvements, it was risky to get to his house. In some places, there was a deep drop of fifty yards or more on the outer side of the narrow road. There would be no room for mistakes, and because of how steep it was, I would have to use a four-wheel drive going down and coming up. Due to Evilazio's work and determination, however, despite the driving challenge, we soon were having meetings in his home.

One late afternoon, we drove to Evilazio's house and preached the Word to the group gathered there, and after the message, as we always did, we invited people to accept the Lord. We left for home after dark, and hadn't gone very far up the mountain before we came upon three huge boulders, blocking the road!

Antonio was a strong Catholic, opposed to Protestants. He had seen us as he was working in his fields as we drove past. In his angry opposition to the gospel, he rolled the boulders onto the road while we were having our meeting. Fortunately, I had another Christian man with me, and the two of us were able to roll these boulders to the side of the road.

Another time, in a different area, while returning at night from a day-long evangelistic trip, a man on a horse, obviously drunk, motioned for us to stop.

"Someone has removed the planks from two bridges up ahead; be careful," he kindly informed us, slurring every word. I wondered, had we crashed through the bridge, would there have been men on hand to attack us?

"Thank you, dear friend, for letting us know about this. You may have saved our lives," I told the man, who continued down the road in his inebriated condition!

I was so glad my co-worker, Glen Bacon, was with me. We stopped the car when we came to the first small bridge, got out and walked over it. Sure enough, several "2 x 12" planks were missing. We found them with no difficulty in the nearby weeds at the side of the road. We put them back in place, and carefully continued to cross the bridge. About a quarter of a mile further on, we came to a much larger bridge. The missing planks from it had been thrown into a deep ditch. These had originally been nailed down with eight-inch spikes: recovering both planks and spikes, and setting them back in place, took a lot more effort than we'd encountered at the first bridge.

Although we never learned for sure who had removed the planks, I suspected one of the farmers who lived nearby to be the ringleader of other men who wanted to do us harm! We did know, however, who had prompted the man on the horse to alert us to danger! *"He will never leave you, or forsake you. Therefore we may boldly say, the Lord is my helper, I will not fear what man can do unto me."* (Hebrews 13:5-6)

Journey to Crixas – Alton was waiting for transportation while on his first trip into the town of Crixas in January 1952.

Crixas Home – Alton, with a friend from the town, at the entrance to their first home in Crixas.

*Dona Francisca – Dona Francisca, a strong believer
and our first landlord, makes soap in a kettle.*

Wedding in Goiania – The wait was finally over!
On July 25, 1952, Alton and Ebba were married in the city of Goiania.

Language School – Mr. and Mrs. Cothron enjoying the sunshine at language school in Campinas, São Paulo in late 1952.

Nonoai Home – Our first home in Nonoai was filled with challenging experiences but held a special place in our hearts.

First Means of Transportation – This bicycle was my first mode of transportation in Nonoai and on the Indian reservation.

*Beatriz in Nonoai – Beatriz plays in front of our second home
in Nonoai that I built a few years earlier.*

*Baptismal Service – A typical baptismal service in the
Uruguay River ca. mid-1960s.*

Indians with Baskets — Baskets and other wares were a source of income for the Indians.

Men's Retreat — Men gather for a men's three-day retreat in Nonoai in the late 1960s.

Language Seminar – Missionaries and Indian informants gather for a month-long language seminar at Rio das Cobras reservation in the state of Parana ca. late 1960s.

Alton with Indian Believers – Precious memories with a Christian Indian and his family who is holding the Gospel According to Mark in Kaingang.

Baptist Church in Nonoai – Thirty years after Alton and Ebba
transitioned to another ministry, the small Baptist Church
founded in Nonoai continued to flourish.

Peniel Home Office – Alton works hard in his office at
Peniel Bible Institute ca. 1970s.

*Family at Peniel – Alton, Ebba, Derly (seated), Arlene,
and Beatriz gather for a family photo in front of their home at the
Peniel Bible Institute ca. 1970s.*

Peniel Staff Members gather for a photo in the late 1970s.

*Peniel Graduation – Family and friends gather for graduation
at Peniel Bible Institute in the early 1980s.*

*Alton and Ebba as Counselors – Alton and Ebba provide counsel
to married students during a return trip to Peniel Bible Institute
after retirement ca. 2005.*

Paulo Carrenho preaches at the Macedonia Bible Institute
Inauguration Service ca. January 1981.

Macedonia Inauguration Service – Many gather for the
inauguration service for the Macedonia Bible Institute near Recife,
Pernambuco in January 1981.

*2nd Story Home at Macedonia – We lived on the second floor
(top left) of this apartment building at Macedonia Bible Institute.*

*Alton and Ebba with Lyle and Louise Denelsbeck –
Lyle and Louise Denelsbeck faithfully served with Alton and Ebba
both in Southern Brazil and at Macedonia Bible Institute.*

*Alton continues to teach Bible studies on a weekly basis
at an assisted living home in Chesapeake, VA.*

CHAPTER TWELVE

CHURCHES PLANTED IN A NO-MAN'S-LAND

*I*t was our hope that one day a church would be planted in Nonoai, despite my first reaction to the village when Floyd Gilbert and I were passing through on a survey trip to determine where to begin working with the Kaingang people. I recall telling Floyd, "What a dismally hot town—dusty roads and unfriendly people. There's a Kaingang Reservation nearby, but I'd never want to live here! This is a no-man's-land!"

But God—He eventually changed my heart, and that is where Ebba and I ended up working for many years! We found that just living and bringing up our children in Nonoai, provided opportunities to share the Gospel. To begin with, however, a few people were unfriendly, hardened against us by the *church* that had held sway in Nonoai since its inception. But as *physical churches* are constructed one brick at a time, so God was using our opportunities, one at a time, to build *His Church* in Nonoai. We began our ministry thwarted at every turn in 1953, but by 1961, there was a group of twenty to thirty people attending services in a little wooden house on the corner close to ours.

Floyd and Ida Gilbert, who recruited us for the Kaingang work in the beginning, had been working with the Kaingang on a reservation near the town of Xanxere. When it was discovered Floyd's tuberculosis had become active again, affecting his spine, under doctor's orders he could no longer carry on strenuous physical activities. The reservation headquarters was about three kilometers from where the Gilberts lived on the boundary of the reservation. They had to cross the Xapecozinho River to reach the reservation.

The Gilberts decided to move to Nonoai in 1959 where he could share the work with me when able, yet rest when it was too painful. A local physician, Dr. Alberto Wunderlich, a close friend of ours, would now treat Floyd's health problems. Though Floyd and Ida's ministries were limited to Nonoai, their daughter Claudette and son Alton would often travel to the Kaingang Reservation with me and help with the literacy classes I was conducting at the time.

We so enjoyed having that year of closeness with the Gilberts, but in October of 1960, Floyd and Ida accepted an invitation to work on loan at a Presbyterian school near the city of São Paulo, and once again, we said goodbye to close friends.

Missionaries are always faced with how to educate their children. Children born abroad generally have dual citizenship status. However, our children were not always considered Brazilian, even though born in Brazil. Nor did they feel American, living so far from grandparents, our supporting churches, and other connections that we had in the United States. We finally decided that Brazil was where our children resided, and that enrolling them in Brazilian schools was best. And so it was, by attending school in Nonoai they became fluent in Portuguese, and kept fluent in English while studying English curriculum with Ebba. This required more hours of schooling each day than their Brazilian classmates, but Ebba made it enjoyable for them, and they seemed to thrive in both schools. When their mother was asked to teach English in the *Ginásio* (equivalent to grades 6-12 in the United States), they were proud to be her children. Ebba was honored to accept the position, and considered it a privilege, and it enhanced our relationship with the people in town.

The Gilberts had built two houses in the jungles across the river from the Xanxere Reservation, knowing that living close to the reservation would be an advantage. The second house was built in anticipation of another missionary family that would be working with them. But now, since they would not be returning, they wanted to sell these houses. They had a young Christian couple living in one of them, who oversaw the Gilberts' properties as caretakers. And these houses turned out to benefit the church group in Nonoai.

When the believers in Nonoai let us know that they wanted to build a church building, we rejoiced! They had outgrown the small house they were using for meetings. I had a suggestion for them, "The Gilberts have two houses they built near the Xanxere Reservation, and they want to sell them. I wonder what you would think about buying those houses, dismantling them, and bringing the lumber and hardware to Nonoai for the church you're planning to build?"

"Find out what the Gilberts want for the houses," was their enthusiastic response.

I thought that first we ought to see the condition of the houses. So, a few of the men from the church and I went in my Jeep to Xanxere, and we found the houses in excellent condition. I let Floyd know our plans, and he sent word back that we could buy the houses, and his price was more than reasonable; in fact, he practically gave them to the church group in Nonoai.

I joined the men who were going to dismantle the houses; with hard work, it took us only a week! We were careful not to damage the lumber and to salvage all the nails and hardware. The dismantling, however, was not the hardest part. Getting the truck into the river valley, loading it, and driving it out again, was challenging! Some of the ceiling and floor joists, which were twenty-one feet long, longer than the bed of the truck, extended over the end of it. On the steepest hill, coming out of the valley, this unsupported weight caused the front end of the truck to rise almost three feet off the ground.

All we could do then was to unload the truck, carry the heavy pieces of lumber up the hill on our backs, and then, reload the truck at the top of the hill. Fortunately, I had driven my jeep out first. I hooked a tow chain onto the truck to help get it up the hill. Let me assure you, unloading and reloading the truck was not a job for sissies!

The men who labored to construct the first Evangelical church building in Nonoai worked for the glory of God. Their cheerfulness and hard work were reminiscent of the determined workers who restored the walls of Jerusalem in the days of Ezra and Nehemiah, who told the people that "*the joy of the Lord is our strength!*"

The dedication of the church was planned for September 30, 1962, and Senhor Luiz Monteiro da Cruz, the president/treasurer of New Tribes Mission of Brazil (*Missão Novas Tribos do Brasil*) agreed to preside over the dedication. The men worked hard to have the building finished in time, and except for a few things they could easily finish later, it showed very well when my good friend Luiz Monteiro da Cruz prayed for the Lord to use the building for His glory, and all who attended services in it from that day forward.

During the ceremony, I couldn't help but remember the early days of our ministry. When we first arrived in Nonoai as Evangelicals, our reception had been on the cool side, as you might remember.

While in Nonoai, Senhor Luis Monteiro da Cruz, stayed in our home with us. I enjoyed taking him around the village and out to the Kaingang Reservation, where he met many of the people with whom we had regular contact. The day he left, I drove him to Erechim, where he boarded a plane back to São Paulo.

About five years after the dedication, the church hired a man to jack up the building several feet and to build a brick basement under the auditorium. Church suppers and other activities were held in the basement. This enlarged building served the Nonoai church until 1987, when a beautiful brick temple replaced it. By this time, the church belonged to the Brazilian Baptist Convention and its first pastor was a former student from the Peniel Bible Institute.

Backing up, I want to write more about our family. In 1955, Dona Maria came to our house with her ten-year-old daughter. (Jack and Joanne Vaughn had taken this girl to raise, but when they left Nonoai to work in the northern part of Brazil, the girl had returned home.) Dona Maria explained her situation. "I am a widow," she began. "And this is my daughter Dalva. When my husband died, he left me alone to raise a house-full of children, and I am struggling to feed and clothe my family. I have thought it over, and have come to ask you to take Dalva and to raise her as your own. That would give her a much better future, and perhaps she could help Ebba in your home."

Taken aback, Ebba and I looked at each other, wondering how we should respond. This would be life-changing, not only for us, but for a ten-year-old that had no say in the decisions being made. How could we refuse? God would give grace to the mother, to Dalva, her siblings, and to us.

We sought counsel from the Justice of the Peace in Nonoai concerning the legal aspects involved. "Adopting is not an option, but I have the authority to grant you legal guardianship. This would give you permission to travel with her, even to take her with you when you return to your own country."

At first, Dalva was insecure and afraid. It was hard: those days were difficult for her and for us. No doubt Dalva wished she could go home, and at times, we wondered if we'd done the right thing. We found out that she was afraid of the dark and would light a candle and keep it burning beside her bed after we were asleep. Our house was a wooden house, with tinder-dry, wooden shingles on the roof. Unattended lighted candles were too dangerous. We could not allow her to continue using them, though she could not understand why.

Little by little, however, we gained her confidence, and when smiles began to appear on her face, we were assured that she was adjusting to her new life. When enrolled in school, Dalva proved to be a good student, very intelligent. At first, Ebba and I could talk to each other in English, knowing that she could not understand, but before long, she was joining in our English conversations!

We left on our first furlough to the United States in 1958, and Dalva went with us. She fit right in with our family. Arlene and Beatriz were so small when she came to live with us, that they accepted her as their big sister. Our parents and friends enjoyed meeting her, and she charmed them with her social graces, and her ability to speak English. After Dalva graduated from high school, she attended and graduated from the Peniel Bible Institute.

Five years after Dalva joined our family, our third child was born, a son this time! He was born on November 11, 1960, in the city of Passo Fundo. He was named after a Brazilian pastor we had met, and whose name we admired. We told each other, "If we ever have a son, let's name him Derly!" And we did!

It had taken a while to let our families in the United States know when our daughters were born—mail is slow, including telegraphs. But this time we had access to a ham radio operator, and through him, we let our families know right away about Derly David Cothron's birth. My father was especially proud to have a grandson! Arlene, Beatriz, and Dalva were good big sisters, and Derly didn't lack attention. As a little boy, he loved making things. The first toys he made were from boxes.

Missionaries living in out-of-the-way places always look forward to annual Field Conferences. Seeing fellow missionaries, hearing about them and their works, and sharing needs and problems with friends is so refreshing. The highlight, though, is the main conference speaker, who in July of 1961 would be Kenneth Johnston, director of the mission.

Anticipating all the above, we piled into our car and set out for the Peniel Bible Institute, a two or three-day trip, where the conference would be held. Because Brazilian members of the mission were also there, the reports and messages were given in Portuguese. I had the privilege of interpreting for Ken as he preached.

At the close of the conference, Ebba and I approached Ken, and invited him to go back to Nonoai with us before heading home. He accepted, and the trip back went faster for us than the trip to the conference. We visited with Ken and pointed things out to him as we traveled. Our five-year-old, Beatriz, was a chatterbox. She sat on Ken's lap and told him story after story throughout the three-day trip: only all the stories were in Portuguese. At first, we tried to tell him what she was saying, but soon gave up and let her jabber away at will. Ken was thoroughly entertained but totally in the dark about the things Beatriz told him. She had a captive audience and was making the most of it. The trip, however, was *punctuated* (literally) by seven flat tires: and one, a blowout!

We detoured at one point of the journey to go by Laranjeiras do Sul, Paraná where the Denelsbecks lived. We didn't stay long, but long enough to make sure the Denelsbecks and Ken had a good visit! Whenever I saw Ken afterward, he would remind me of how much he enjoyed the trip he took with us after the field conference.

CHAPTER THIRTEEN

REINFORCEMENTS

*I*n August of 1961, Glen and Shirley Bacon came to Nonoai and joined us in the Kaingang work. They had four children, so we had quite a houseful for a few weeks, until they found a house to rent. Eventually, they obtained permission to live on the Kaingang Reservation. We worked very well together, and it was wonderful to finally have missionaries living among the Kaingang. Shirley served as a midwife for some of the women, which gave her many opportunities to show God's love and to present the gospel to them.

The Gospel Recordings Network (GRN) has played a very significant role in producing audio-visual materials for the least-reached language groups of the world! In December of 1961, two men from the network arrived in Nonoai. Glen Bacon and I spent a week with them, making tapes of Bible messages in the Kaingang language. One of the Kaingang men, who spoke Portuguese as well as his own language, was on hand to help us translate the messages into current, normal Kaingang. We worked outside under the shade of a big tree. In the succeeding years, we used these taped messages a lot. I would take my battery-powered tape recorder everywhere, and the people showed a lot of interest in listening to the messages in their own tongue.

We also were given messages recorded by GRN in the Guarani language, the tribe that shared the reservation with the Kaingang. Occasionally, we made the difficult trip, roads and distance being what they were, into the area where the Guarani lived. Though we did not speak their language, we could evangelize them by playing the GRN messages for them.

Another couple that came to help with the Kaingang work was Francisco Alves and his wife, Olga. They had been students at the Evangelical Missionary Institute (*Instituto Evangélico Missionário*), which later became known as the *Instituto Bíblico Peniel.*

The little town of Planalto was on the far west side of the Kaingang Reservation, and I was sure that would be a good place for the Alveses to work. The town itself was very strongly opposed to Evangelicals, a lot like Nonoai was when we first arrived. Francisco and Olga could provide the evangelistic witness that was needed, and could also make visits to the western part of the Kaingang Reservation which, because of its location, was difficult for me to reach with the gospel.

We located a small wooden house in Planalto for Francisco and Olga to rent and helped them set up housekeeping. We loaned them a young cow for milk. Their living conditions were not *fancy*, but in keeping with those of the people in the area.

Right from the start, Francisco was a good evangelist and witnessed to everyone. One of our objectives as we worked with the Kaingang People was to teach people to read and write. For any future church to thrive it was necessary that its members be able to read. With literacy in mind, Francisco made a trip to Porto Alegre, the capital of the state of Rio Grande do Sul. He went to purchase educational materials and books for the classes he planned to have. He took his five-year-old boy with him.

It was an all-day trip on a bus over dirt roads until they ran into paving near to the city. Francisco was invited to stay with the janitor of a church, whose living quarters were in the church building. That night, Francisco died in his sleep. What we did not know, until later, was that he had an enlarged heart due to Chagas disease. Chagas disease is transmitted by insects and only found in rural areas of Latin America where poverty is widespread, and rarely does the person infected know he has the disease and that his heart is being damaged.

The next morning, the janitor discovered him dead. Word of Francisco's death was radioed to Planalto by the police department, but the message was very brief. The address of Francisco's whereabouts and details of his death were not clear. Dona Olga found someone to bring her from Planalto to our house in Nonoai.

Ebba and I were not at home when Olga arrived. We had been in the city of Erechim, had driven home at night in a downpour of rain, and arrived home to find Olga waiting for us. The next day, Glen Bacon, Ebba, Dona Olga, and I drove to Porto Alegre. We arrived there about 11:00 in the evening. We spent two hours checking with hospitals, first aid clinics, and, with the police, trying to locate where Francisco's body was, but to no avail. Exhausted, we finally went to a hotel to get a little rest. The next day we continued our search.

Finally, with the aid of a local pastor, we located the church where Francisco had died. The people there were just getting ready to take the body to the cemetery for burial. We accompanied them, and at the cemetery, I preached a short graveside message. The little boy was reunited with his mother, and that same afternoon we began our long journey back to Nonoai. Dona Olga was expecting another child within a few weeks, so she stayed with us in Nonoai until their child was born.

Olga was, of course, still in mourning, attempting to comfort and calm her little son, and wondering what she would do now after her baby came. But life goes on. One day, she washed their clothes and hung them on the barbed wire fence that enclosed our cattle. A cow pulled Olga's dress off the fence and proceeded to chew it to pieces! We would have made a joke of it under other circumstances, but now, it seemed just too much for Olga to bear! Ebba was quick to comfort her, and went with her to buy cloth for another dress!

But the tragedy was not over. After Olga recovered from the birth of her baby, she boarded a bus with her children, and traveled to Vianopolis, in the state of Goias where our Mission Headquarters was located. About that same time, I arranged for a truck to take her belongings to Vianópolis. Olga found a job teaching, and after a time she remarried. Unfortunately, the second marriage did not go well, and Olga died a tragic death at the hands of her husband.

A few years passed before another missionary couple took up the work in Planalto where the Alveses had been. George and Bonnie Nelson arrived and continued the work that Francisco had begun in town on the west side of the Kaingang Reservation.

Later the Nelsons were given permission to build a house on the reservation. I helped him with the construction of the house, and that is where George and Bonnie lived while working with the Kaingang for four years. Their children were at home only part of the year as they attended the Mission boarding school in Vianopolis.

Both Kaingang and Brazilian townspeople were saved through George's ministry, and some are firm believers to this day. One of these is Dona Leticia. She is now quite elderly but firm in her faith. Another was João Ferreira, who I had the privilege of baptizing in the small river on the west side of Nonoai during a retreat for men. It was very moving to see Joao, a seventy-two-year-old man, climbing slowly down the bank into the water and to see his tears of joy as he came up out of the water.

An annual three-day men's Bible conference and retreat was being held in Nonoai at this time and João was one of those present. Many years later, after Ebba and I had left the Kaingang work, we returned to Planalto for a visit and learned that João Ferreira was still alive. Dona Leticia knew where he lived and took us to see him. He was over ninety years of age and living by himself in a little wooden house on the edge of town; his wife, who was not a Christian, had died several years before. He was very deaf, and it was difficult for him to hear or see. But once he recognized me, he beamed all over. He showed me that he still had his Bible. After a short visit and prayer we left, sad that he lived in such deplorable living conditions! I knew I would never see him alive again on this earth.

Ursula Weismann of the Summer Institute of Linguistics lived and worked at the Rio das Cobras Kaingang Reservation, located in the southwestern part of the state of Paraná. She was working on the translation of the New Testament, and had developed materials for teaching Kaingang. In May of 1967 Miss Weismann invited missionaries from three or four missions to participate in an in-depth study of the Kaingang language. Glen Bacon and I took advantage of the month-long course. Each participant had to bring along a Kaingang language informant to assist him. Winter was setting in: it would be cool.

The language helper that Glen and I took with us from Nonoai was João Carlos, a quick, intelligent person. When we approached him about accompanying us to the month-long course, he accepted right away. Living conditions were very simple. I slept on the floor in a sleeping bag which proved to be none too warm on those cold, fall winter nights. We had two choices for bathing. There was a small river that circled the back side of the property where the post headquarters buildings were located. The only problem was the water was icy cold! The other option was to haul water and put it in a shower can inside a small wooden shower house. This way you could heat your water ahead of time. Meals were served in a make-shift kitchen/dining room. In the morning, we were taught grammar, followed by time with our informant, to work on pronunciation. Afternoons were spent visiting Kaingang homes to practice what we were learning. There were simple church services each day. Ursula had a way of pushing us to our limits, determined that the outcome of the course would be greater fluency in the language that she spoke so well. One special event during this month in Rio das Cobras was a baptismal service held in the icy cold waters of the small river mentioned above.

Both Kaingang and Guarani can be found on the Kaingang Reservations. The chief of the Guarani group came to see Ursula one day, and asked her to send a team of missionaries to the Guarani side of the reservation to treat the sick. I volunteered to take my Jeep station wagon. A date was set, and about six of us, including a missionary nurse, left for the Guarani area, two hours away. The dirt road was in poor condition and finally became narrower and narrower until there was no road at all. We left the car parked under the shade of a large tree near a farmhouse and walked the last four kilometers. As we arrived at the village, the people set off fireworks. At first, we thought it was to welcome us, but later discovered the real reason for the fireworks was to signal people living a distance from the village. Soon people were coming from all directions.

We set up shop, so to speak, out in the open and spent the next four hours taking care of kids and adults with colds, dysentery, cuts, burns, and other ailments. What a time we had! It was around four o'clock in the afternoon before we could take a break and eat lunch. Fast forwarding: Wycliffe (SIL) missionaries have since worked with this group of Guarani People and today there are many believers and a church.

On another day, while on the Rio das Cobras Reservation, I was asked to take one of the Kaingang families to the hospital some twenty-five miles away. This sounds simple and almost routine, right? Well, it was anything but: it had to do with a twelve-year-old girl, who had never ridden in a vehicle! To say she was scared to death, is to put it mildly. Neither had she ever left the reservation, plus the terms of *hospital* and *doctor* were terrifying to her.

The poor girl's feet were swollen with infection and the itching was unbearable! She was suffering from a condition called *bicho de pe* (feet penetrated by a small tropical flea called *tunga*). The *tunga flea* is invisible to the eye. When the fertile female penetrates the skin of the person, a small egg sack develops with the little flea inside it. Until it is removed, it multiplies rapidly, causing itching. The sack must be removed intact: flea and all, probing for it with a sterilized sewing needle.

When the doctor saw my little passenger's feet, he said, "We can't take them all out in one day, there are too many. She will have to return another day to finish the job. She must return, and if she doesn't, she could die.

The little girl was frantic—she cried and screamed as the doctor probed her feet. Her parents, who saw and heard all, refused to take her back to the doctor. Later, I heard that the child died a few months after that visit to the doctor.

So you see, along with our studies, we were called upon to help the Kaingang in all sorts of situations, and returned home, our heads full of the intricacies of this challenging language!

Our teacher, Ursula Weissman, came to Nonoai to see us several times before and after the language course, and stayed anywhere from a few days to a week or more on these visits. Since she was still working on the translation of the New Testament into Kaingang, we discussed many things concerning her translation work, and let her know we were happy to help in any way we could. Ebba and I made numerous trips with her to other reservations for the purpose of checking the translations. There were four dialects in the Kaingang language, which complicated the checking. It was necessary to verify what words served best for a particular reservation. Ursula was a very dedicated and focused worker, admired by all.

Ebba stayed home in Nonoai, while I took the month-long course over two hundred miles away. Besides our three children, she had the care of one of the Bacon's children also. I prayed much that none of the kids would get sick while I was gone. On other occasions, Ebba had to deal with sick children while I was away, which was very hard for her. There was no telephone service in those days. She couldn't let me know anything, and I couldn't call to check on her. This time, God answered my prayers, and I found everyone healthy and Ebba functioning well when I returned home, eager to share with her the things I had learned.

Missionaries working with tribal people in Brazil work under government agencies. One of them, the SPI (Indian Protective Service), founded in 1910, began with noble intentions, but had become corrupt, so we were told, and was no longer doing its job. So, in 1967 the SPI was abolished, and a new agency called FUNAI (National Indigenous People Foundation) took its place. As missionaries, we tried to cooperate with these agencies without becoming involved in their politics or interfering with their functions. Sometimes, this was difficult. Not all the Kaingang Post Inspectors working with these agencies looked kindly on missionary efforts. We were always on our toes to maintain good relationships with them.

Another thing that concerned us missionaries in the 1960s was the rapid spread of tuberculosis throughout the Kaingang nation, a vast area from northern Paraná to northern Rio Grande do Sul. We treated some of the Kaingang who had contracted TB on the Nonoai Reservation. There was little improvement, and eventually, a couple of them were taken to a hospital in Porto Alegre for treatment. Though we encouraged the Kaingang to take the medications faithfully and to improve their diets, they were not always cooperative. The concept of invisible germs, and how they spread the disease to others, was lost on them, as were our teachings about how good hygiene could protect their families from the contagion.

The reservation headquarters had a small, poorly equipped clinic, and the Kaingang had little faith in going there. I would sometimes take people there in my vehicle if they were too weak to walk. One lady had waited too long to seek treatment, as was the case with many. I drove her and her baby to the reservation headquarters to begin treatment, though it was plain that she was too sick to pull through. A few days later, I was asked to take the lady back to her house in the jungle, and told, "She wants to die at home."

We drove as close as we could to her residence, then, four of us men, carried her on a blanket into her house. One of our co-workers, Maria José Cardoso, a single lady who was a teacher, went to see her that same day and talked to her about salvation, but that night, the lady died. Was she saved? Had the Holy Spirit brought understanding and faith to her heart? Our job was to tell the story of Jesus. It was God's to bring the increase. This knowledge has kept us from asking certain questions, and from becoming discouraged by not knowing the answers.

The father of the lady who had succumbed to tuberculosis was a friend of mine. Everyone knew him by his nickname: Chico Flauta. At one time, many years ago, the Kaingang played flutes (flautas). But now, the flutes they made were just artifacts that were sold to Brazilians to gain a little money. From the time when I came on the scene, Chico Flauta was the only one I ever knew who still knew how to play these native flutes: the music was minor, and tended to put one in a melancholy mood. Sad to say, Chico Flauta was a drunkard, and on various occasions, I found him lying in the weeds alongside the road, sleeping it off.

One day, however, I found Chico Flauta sober when I went to his little hut in the woods. He seemed glad to see me and opened his heart to me. He said, "Sr. Alton, I don't have anything in this world! I am not respected, and it is all because of drinking. I go to the store to buy salt, sugar, or flour, and I don't want to buy drink, but something inside pulls me to do so, and I end up spending my money on liquor." I pointed Chico Flauta to Christ and shared scripture with him more than once, trusting his soul to Jesus.

CHAPTER FOURTEEN

GROWING PAINS

*B*esides helping the Kaingang with their health needs, we knew that helping them to read would give them a foot up in becoming respected by the people outside the reservation. But most of all, we wanted them to read so that they could read God's Word.

We were thrilled in the 1960's when two single lady missionaries, graduates of the *Instituto Biblico Peniel*, came to assist in the work among the Kaingang. One of them, Maria Azevedo, a lady in her mid-forties, took over the little school for Kaingang children, at the reservation headquarters. She had a sewing machine, and besides teaching children to read and write, she taught a few of the girls and women to sew.

I made weekly trips to Maria's house, taking supplies for her and the school. At times, Ebba would go to the reservation with me, and she and Maria would visit the homes of her students, some of which lived as far as two miles away.

Maria wanted to expand the world view of the Kaingang students to include being true citizens of Brazil. One way that she did this was teaching her students to sing the Brazilian National Anthem. Another way was by obtaining permission for the Kaingang students to march with the Brazilian students in the Brazilian Independence Day parade in the town of Nonoai. Her efforts were successful, and increased the moral of the Kaingang students and their parents.

Eventually Maria José Cardoso moved to a location known as the Bananeiras, six kilometers from the post headquarters at the Nonoai Reservation. It was known that there were many Kaingang children in that area that needed schooling, and the SPI (Indian Protective Service) had begun the construction of a small house and a school building for this cause. The buildings were never finished, perhaps due to a lack of funds.

I offered to finish the construction of the house and school building and to put a teacher there. The post director had become good friends with us by this time, and he was happy with my offer and willing to cooperate by furnishing the lumber to finish the schoolhouse and living quarters.

It only took a few days for Glen Bacon and me to finish the buildings, which were made of rough lumber with wooden shingles for roofing. We cleaned up all around the buildings and were planning to take Maria José early the next morning to move into her new living quarters. I had counted about sixty-five children as potential students although I did not expect that many would turn up for school.

The morning after the clean-up, I went to buy some stove pipe that we needed to set up the wood cook stove for Maria. As I was walking by the bus station, I met Chico Forte, a Kaingang man that I knew. He had just gotten off the bus, and he said, "Have you heard about the school building and house in Bananeiras? It burned to the ground last night?" I was shocked and said to Chico, "Are you kidding me?" He assured me he was not kidding! I hurried home to tell Ebba, Glen and Shirley, and Maria about it.

I suggested we drive out to Bananeiras and see for ourselves what had happened. Arriving there, we were shocked to find only ashes, bent nails and some balls of glass where windowpanes had been, and a few Kaingang people that had gathered.

Our minds could not take it in! How did this happen? Who did it? Why? The answer to these questions was never known! I suspected an individual who lived nearby, but there was no way to prove he was the guilty one. The Lord knew all about who did it and what his motives were! We left it in His hands.

Suffice it to say, we felt led to rebuild! The director of the Kaingang Reservation was of the same mind and again furnished the lumber; Glen and I supplied the rest of the material and the labor. Others joined with us, even some of the Kaingang men, and the school was soon rebuilt! Instead of two buildings, we decided to construct one large building. The classroom was in front, and an apartment for the teachers behind. It was not fancy, but was quite livable. Lamps were used for light, and a well was dug for water. Later, we planted fruit trees and shade trees.

Things rapidly fell into place. Maria moved into her apartment, the stove was set up, her bed was made, and she prepared the schoolroom for classes. She didn't have desks for the students yet, but school was up and running: the memory of the destruction of the original buildings faded into the background.

Many Kaingang children learned to read and write in this little school. They were soon singing the National Anthem with pride and hearing the Gospel, some for the very first time. One of the little girls who studied in this school is now married, a mother of several children and a missionary, along with her husband, to her own people. She and her husband, Hélio, studied at the Jacutinga Bible School. They are good friends of ours, and Ebba and I have visited them a few times.

Over the years, I taught quite a few Kaingang adults to read one-on-one. This meant going to their homes on the reservation, traveling either by bicycle, vehicle, or on foot. These one-on-one sessions to teach reading opened opportunities to share the gospel, and helped me to improve my ability to speak Kaingang, as I interacted with my Kaingang students.

After every session, I would let them know when I would return to continue our studies. I would honor my plans, only to find some students not at home when I arrived. Neighbors would tell me, "Oh, he's out working in his fields." I'd check it out, and find him hoeing corn, or pulling up beans. "Or he may have gone to the store to buy things he and his family need," they'd tell me, "Such as salt, flour, or cloth." Sometimes, a relative was ill and the Kaingang student had gone to see him. Motivation was low and, in some instances, non-existent, but I persevered and over the years some did learn to read!

Not all the Kaingang parents saw schooling as important, either for themselves or for their children. When I asked one man if his children would be attending school, he put a question to me, "What will you pay me to send my two boys to school?" And he followed with, "Tell me, how can learning to read and write help them to live any better? Will it make them better farmers?"

In the end, he did send his boys to school, and they were doing well until a tragedy took place. One of the boys was hit and killed by a passing truck while returning home from school one afternoon. The father became very bitter and took the other son out of school.

Despite the difficulties and discouragement, we continued to make literacy a priority. The system we used was to teach people to read first in Kaingang, and when they could read well in their own language, we would transition them to reading Portuguese. This system has proven to be the best one for ethnic groups who need and want to learn the trade language to fit into the social and economic structure of the country they live in.

At first Ebba could not go with me to the Kaingang Reservation, but when the children were older, we visited it as a family. We wanted our children to learn about our work in the best way—by participating in it. The Kaingang people loved to see Ebba and our kids. They were pleased to have Arlene and Beatriz helping them learn to read and write! In 1967, when Ebba was carrying our fourth child, one of the men, in anticipation of its birth, made a Kaingang baby basket for her. Alberto was an old man who had retained the skill of weaving with bamboo.

We were all excited to welcome the new baby into our home, but it was not to be. Our baby died at birth due to RH Negative complications. The Kaingang people mourned with us. They observed that we were vulnerable human beings just like they: our children could die, too. This brought us even closer to them.

The first baptismal service held for the Kaingang in the Nonoai Reservation was a long time coming! And the first one we baptized, João Pedro, was one of the men I had taught to read. His wife and two of his children were also baptized that day in the small stream that flowed through the valley and behind the sawmill. We searched along the stream, and finally located a big hole where the water was deep enough for the baptism. Our co-worker, Vladimir Salmin, did the baptizing.

Immediately after the baptism, a group of us followed João Pedro and his family home for a communion service. On the way it began to rain, and we were soaked by the time we reached the house. But it didn't dampen our spirits at all as we celebrated communion, also a first for the Kaingang!

João Pedro struggled to quit smoking, and would try to hide it when he'd succumb to his craving, and light up one of his hand-rolled 'cornhusk cord tobacco cigarettes.' One day, I stopped by the sawmill where he worked. He was feeding firewood into the boiler that powered the sawmill. He didn't see me arriving and had his back to me, and because of the noise of the machinery, he didn't hear me right away! When he did, realizing it was I, he snatched the cigarette he was smoking from his mouth in one swoop, and held it tightly in his closed fist. I could see by the contortions of his face both that he was ashamed, and that his fist was being burned! I told him, "João Pedro, I am going to ask the Lord to make smoking so distasteful to you, that you will want to quit!"

God must have heard my prayer, because a few weeks later I saw his wife, and with delight, she told me, speaking in Kaingang, "Joao Pedro despises the taste of tobacco, and has stopped smoking. One day he took his cornhusks and tobacco and threw them into the fire!"

Teaching people to read produced two positive results. First, it was a great help to me in learning more of the language. I found that the Kaingang that were highly motivated to read, were also highly motivated to correct me when I said something incorrectly. Second, because we used Scripture as reading material, our students were being evangelized along with gaining fluency in reading.

The first reading primers, developed by SIL, were simple, as were the workbooks for teaching writing, and we used these for people just getting started. Later, small booklets on health and hygiene, and other topics were also produced for practice in reading. The tape recorder became a useful tool, and the Kaingang would listen to lessons and messages on tape. And we gradually introduced them to reading Scripture.

João Cadete was one of my Kaingang students, who also became a good language helper. He was not a fast learner, but was faithful. His brother Francisco was a better student, but was not as faithful as João. When João reached the point where he could read well enough, he read to me from the Gospel of Mark and the Epistle of Titus. He became a believer and a preacher of the Gospel. Though I lost track of João when he joined a Pentecostal group that formed in the Kaingang Reservation, he is a good example of how slow learners can eventually learn to read and write through faithful practice!

Gumercindo, the Kaingang chief, mentioned earlier in the book, eventually turned his position as chief over to a younger man, and moved away from the Post Headquarters. He was older and in poor health at this point, and never travelled far from home. I visited him often, and would read to him from the Gospel of Mark. When we came to the account of the crucifixion, Gumercindo was very moved, and I believe this was what brought him to salvation.

In February of 1969, I heard that Gumercindo was very ill and not expected to live. I went to his house, and it was plain to see that my dear friend was near death. Family members were gathering to be with him. He was lying on a mat, clean and dressed in a new shirt. When Gumercindo saw me, he sat up despite his weakness. We began to talk, and he said, "I believe in God, I believe in Jesus, but I would like to have my health back." A little later, he addressed all of us who were gathered around him, and said: "Bow your heads and close your eyes, now we're going to pray." He wanted me to pray. Our hearts were touched, to say the least. Though Gumercindo had refused all medication or offers to be taken to the Post Headquarters, he finally agreed to take some medication. Vladimir, who had come with me to see Gumercindo, left us and went to get medication for him. When he returned, over an hour later, he gave Gumercindo an injection: to no avail. Soon after, Gumercindo passed away and although I can't be certain of his salvation there are good indications he was saved. His refusal to seek medical help was typical of the Kaingang, who had little faith in the white man's medicines! Their belief, for the most part, was in their tribal shamans.

I came to know one of these shamans quite well. Velho Ricardo (*Old Richard*) could only walk with the aid of a cane or holding onto something. "Many years ago I fell off a horse," he told me, "And I have been crippled ever since." He was always at home when I came to visit him, and despite his disability, Old Ricardo was jolly and loved to tell jokes, so I will tell a few about him. I think his last bath must have been prior to his fall from the horse! I'm sure he never washed his hair, but despite the dirt, it was still black, and he had lots of it! (Go figure, I take care of my hair, and end up bald, and what little I have is turning grey!) Ricardo smiled and laughed a lot, and when he did, you could see he only had two or three teeth in his mouth.

Old Ricardo earned his living by being the village shaman. The Kaingang would come to him, and after telling Old Ricardo their health concern, he would tell them, "I can prepare just the right medicine to give you." He would charge a small fee for the "medicine" he prescribed. The concoction might include leaves, roots, ashes, water, and only God knows what else, and were taken without any concern about its sanitation.

I generally tried to slip up on Old Ricardo, without him hearing or seeing me, although that was difficult because all Kaingang have dogs! Even so, Ricardo would invariably greet me with, "I knew you would be here today, because I had a dream last night that you would come." My visits, of course, had nothing to do with his being a shaman, but being a soul for whom Christ died! I would explain the Gospel to Old Ricardo and to whoever might be there, awaiting his *prescription*.

Knowing that Jesus promised to build His Church and that nothing could prevent it, gave us the perseverance needed to keep on preaching to the Kaingang, regardless of whether our message was received or not.

Perseverance pays, however! And faith is the victory that overcomes the world! By the late 1960s, we were having services with a group of Kaingang on a regular basis. A little church was forming. We did not yet have all the New Testament, but used what we had, trusting that Ursula Weismann would one day complete it. We preached from Mark, Titus, Acts, and portions of the book of Genesis.

I'll never forget the day a truck stopped at the door of our house and unloaded several boxes with a total of six hundred copies of the Gospel of Mark in the Kaingang language. I thought, "We *must* teach Kaingang people to read! Until we have readers, we cannot distribute these books indiscriminately."

The mimeographed copies of the first Kaingang hymnbook contained sixteen hymns and choruses. With the passing of years, the number grew to over a hundred songs. In our group of believers, João Pedro became the song leader. He always led off with songs pitched so high, that, of necessity, others had to sing in lower ranges resulting in inharmonious singing. It did not bother the Kaingang nearly as much as us missionaries; however, no doubt it was *a sweet, sweet sound to God's ears* as Kaingang believers made their joyful *noise* to the Lord.

Little by little, Kaingang literature began to accumulate! Eventually, we had a set of nine literacy primers we used to teach the Kaingang to read! And once they could read, a little at a time, new material in their language would be written! Some Kaingang were very intelligent and learned to read quickly. Some were average, and others took a little longer. Some just could not learn, but these were generally good listeners!

Both the Kaingang believers and believers in Nonoai, as they grew in their walks with the Lord, became servants as well as believers, sharing Christ with their friends and relatives. Hopefully, we modeled this for them, and joined with them whenever we could in their outreach to lead people to the Lord. This was the case with Evilazio, a Christian man from near Nonoai. He desired to lead his brother to the Lord who lived in Caxambu, a small town in the neighboring State of Santa Catarina, a trip of less than 25 miles from Nonoai. Evilazio recruited Glen Bacon and me to take him to visit his brothers—this involved crossing the Uruguay River on a ferry.

We received a warm welcome from Evilazio's brother and his family when we arrived, and in true Brazilian fashion, we were served a delicious dinner. In the afternoon, we gathered in front of the house to hold a preaching service. There was no shade, and the sun was still shining relentlessly when I began my message. I used Isaiah 53 for my text. Though Jesus is not mentioned explicitly in this Old Testament passage, it describes him so well that there is no doubt that the *sin-bearer* it talks about is Jesus. The main road passed right in front of the house, and some of those passing by stopped to hear the message. Another of Evilazio's brothers, named Manoel, arrived on horseback soon after I'd started preaching. Manoel lived a couple of miles away. As soon as I finished preaching, he bid us goodbye, mounted his horse and rode away without any comment on the message.

However, two or three weeks later, Manoel came knocking on our door in Nonoai. He said, "My family and I have decided to become believers in Christ, and I have come to buy a Bible and a hymn book." It was rare, in our experience, to see people come to Christ after only one exposure to the Gospel, but the Lord had used this meaningful passage of scripture in Isaiah to make real to Manoel why Jesus had suffered on the cross. We continued to visit them and to disciple them in the Christian life, and I had the privilege of baptizing most of them. The beautiful thing is he and his family have been firm in the faith for over forty years.

Soon after Manoel's visit to purchase a Bible and hymnal, he, his wife Isaltina, and their children moved to a new farm over sixty miles north. It was very near a new and growing town by the name of Campo Erê. Knowing that there was no Evangelical church in Campo Erê where Manoel's family could fellowship and receive teaching, Ebba and I began going to visit them the last weekend of every month. This was a six-to-seven-hour trip on a dirt road, which was either dusty or muddy and always rough, winding over beautiful mountains and through valleys covered with fields of corn, beans, or wheat.

On these visits to Manoel, we contacted and evangelized many other families. I always took with me a good supply of gospel tracts, and as we traveled to and from Campo Erê, we'd throw tracts to people walking along the road and in the towns as we passed through. People scrambled to pick up the tracts.

We always wondered what happened when the tracts were read! Then one day we learned what happened to at least one man: Amador Moreira! He knew our car since we would often pass by his house on our way to Campo Erê. One day as we were winding down the mountain road, Amador flagged us down. I stopped, rolled down the window of the car, and this is what he told us: "I work for the State Highway Department doing maintenance, cutting weeds, and cleaning out culverts, and whenever you passed by, you'd thrown tracts at me from your car. That's why I wanted you to stop today; I wanted you to know that after I read the tracts, I received Christ as my Savior and I want you to baptize me."

In April of 1969, during a men's retreat in Nonoai, I had the privilege of baptizing Amador Moreira in the river that flowed near the house of another Christian family. Amador's wife also made a profession of faith, though we could not be sure her conversion was real, or whether it was done to please her husband. Later Amador moved far away to work in a sawmill, and I lost contact with him.

In 1972, the Lord opened a new door and we moved from Nonoai, but left behind scattered believers and groups of believers, still struggling, and growing.

CHAPTER FIFTEEN

COMBINING EFFORTS, SOWING SEEDS

*L*yle and Louise, and Delbert and Madeline Denelsbeck had been working in the Laranjeiras do Sul, Parana area for quite a few years. They were good friends of ours who we didn't see all that often, because they lived quite a distance from us. We had heard about the yearly retreats for youth they were having, and when they invited us to bring young people from the Nonoai area, we were delighted.

After the young people from Nonoai joined those of the Parana area, there were close to a hundred young people in attendance. One thing we insisted on was that the young people themselves should earn the money to pay for the retreats. Most accepted the challenge: some earned the money by working for their parents, and others found work outside their homes in their communities, among them our own daughters, Arlene and Beatriz.

A lot of planning went into the youth retreats. One event followed another so that the young people were kept busy and challenged! There was always a special speaker, time set aside for memorizing Bible verses, and times for games and sports. At the end of each retreat, we would assign a book of the Bible to be read and studied in preparation for the following year. To stir up interest, we'd tell them: "There's going to be a competition among all the youth groups next year to see which group can answer the most questions correctly about the book that you'll be studying!"

Twice when the retreat was held in Parana, we had so many young people going from Nonoai we had to charter a bus.

Not only did we plan the events, but we also had to address the matters of food, utensils, equipment, retreat personnel, and other things, so that when the big day arrived everything would be ready, and things would run smoothly. We also knew just who would do what!

Ebba and I oversaw bringing the dishes and utensils one year. I spoke to the owner of a store in Nonoai, and asked him if he could help. He agreed to provide the dishes, and said: "Return them to me after the retreat, and I'll only charge you for those that are broken!" And what seemed a miracle, as I recall, when we returned them to the generous storekeeper, none of the dishes had been broken. These retreats were a lot of work, but well worth it, not only was a good time had by all, but many of the young people grew serious about following the Lord, and studying his Word.

In the late 1960s we began to have retreats for men as well as for youth: working again with the Denelsbeck's. We decided that the men's retreats would be held in Parana one year, and in Nonoai the next. The purpose for the men's retreats was to train Christian men to become leaders in their local church fellowships, the by-product at the retreat was the fellowship: men relating to each other, blessing, and encouraging one other. Because men could not be away from their farms or jobs for longer periods of time, the retreats were only three days long. But these days were packed full!

In the morning sessions, we had Bible study, preaching, and a prayer time. In the afternoons, the men went out by twos or threes to assigned locations to preach, teach, and evangelize. At night, we gathered again for an evening meeting with helpful messages for our personal walk with God, and how to reach people with the gospel. Generally, there were men who wanted to be baptized, and the baptismal services at those retreats with only men present were extremely heart-warming.

The men's retreats, though they lasted only three days, still required much coordination and planning. The fact that the men brought all the food themselves, cut down considerably on what they had to pay to attend. One would bring rice, another beans, another meat, and one time, they even provided the cook! When the retreat was held in Nonoai, a lady who lived out of town, got behind the retreat, and made bread, and sent it to us each day on the bus.

One year, the young people's retreat was held on Senhor Maneco Lopes' farm near Porto Santana in the state of Parana. We had lots of rain during the retreat, which worried Senhor Maneco. His farm was a few miles off the main road, and a dirt road led to it. When he checked it out at the end of the retreat, he knew the chartered bus from Nonoai would not be able to get to the farm because of the mud! He decided to load all of us from Nonoai into his truck and drive us out to the main road, but the mud was so deep at one spot, the truck got stuck. There was a bulldozer beside the road, but no one knew how to run it. Everyone was praying. And the time to meet our bus on the main road grew closer and closer. Suddenly, we heard a vehicle. Soon, a jeep came into view, stopped, and a man got out to see if he could help us. We learned that he was authorized to operate the bulldozer! He got it going, hooked a big chain onto the truck, and pulled us all the way out to the main road. Believe me, there were lots of cheers and hallelujahs when we arrived: just in time!

For so long, during the early days of our ministry in Nonoai, we wondered when or if we would see believers. Now, not only were people accepting Christ, but requesting to be baptized as well! The baptismal services were always a major event as well as a challenge. Because few large rivers exist in southern Brazil, the baptisms took place wherever we found enough water: in streams, small rivers, or ponds.

I remember well the first man I baptized, who lived three miles from our house. His name was Evilazio, a big man over six feet tall. The Passo Fundo River in front of his house was fast-flowing, and that is where I was going to baptize him. Evilazio and I entered the water and waded out to a point deep enough, yet not in a strong current, or so we thought. Footing was difficult because of the rocky bottom of the river. As I laid Evilazio back in the water to baptize him, the current swept us both away. Yes, it was funny, and we all had a good laugh, but in the end, the baptism was successfully performed. I baptized quite a few people near that same spot later, but not without remembering Evilazio's baptism and wondering what might happen!

During the early years in Nonoai, not only did we wonder when, if ever, there would be believers, but when there were believers, would they ever construct church buildings on their own? One of the important things we had learned in missionary training was that the believers needed to be self-propagating, not dependent on the missionary, which was proof that you'd done your job well. When we saw this very thing happening, we were so pleased!

Senhor Leopoldo and Dona Antonia lived 20 miles west of Nonoai near the Uruguay River. Weather permitting, every two weeks, we'd drive there on Sunday afternoons for house-to-house visitation and preaching services. After a time, the group in attendance at our preaching services grew to forty or fifty people. We began meeting in a garage-like structure down the hill from a farmhouse, but later, Leopoldo and some of the other men built a small church on his property on a hilltop with a good view of the surrounding area.

Having enough water was not the problem when a group of seventeen people from Senhor Leopoldo's church group asked to be baptized: the Uruguay River was over 400 yards wide at this point! One problem did exist, however. The riverbanks were very steep and the bottom of the river very muddy. There was no good footing anywhere for people to get in and out of the water. Just days before the baptism, which had been scheduled for a Sunday afternoon, the Lord sent a good hard rain which caused a huge portion of the high steep bank to break loose and fall into the river, forming a small island that I could stand on, even though I sank nearly to my knees in the mud while baptizing. We made a wooden path with planks, and one by one, those who would be baptized climbed atop the island. It was a memorable day, and we thanked the Lord for the rain that broke the steep bank loose, and made the baptism safe and possible, though the baptizer and the baptized all left the river covered with mud!

We were just finishing the church service one evening when a man came in and sat down at the back of the room. As we were packing up our things to leave, he asked for a ride into Nonoai. The car was already full since Delbert and Madeline Denelsbeck were with us, but we talked it over and decided we'd make room for the stranger. He sat up front with me, and the whole way he slouched down with his hat pulled over his face. As I drove the twenty-five kilometers into town, I tried talking to our mysterious passenger. His answers were a mixture of yes or no, and grunts. When we arrived on the edge of town he said, "Let me out at the corner." We did, and he disappeared into the darkness.

The next morning, we learned he had killed a man not far from the church on Senhor Leopoldo's property, and had hidden in the church as he was fleeing the area. We could see the headlines now: Missionaries Help Criminal Escape!

Pedro and Isaltina Ferreira, a family that seemed prone to *hard times,* struggled to make a living, farming the steep, rocky hillsides on one side of the Passo Fundo River. They had chickens, and as hard as it was to get the eggs to Nonoai, he would take them there to sell where there were more customers and where he'd get a better price for them. One day, he carefully rolled several dozen eggs in corn husks and placed them in a bag over the back of his horse behind the saddle. All went well till he arrived at our house. He left the horse loose in our front yard, walked up to the house to see how many eggs we wanted, and just when he turned to get the eggs, the horse, tired from the long journey, decided to lay down and roll over! We didn't get to purchase any eggs from Pedro that day. You guessed it, when he retrieved the bag, it was one big omelet!

Despite all their hard times, however, the Ferreiras and all their children became faithful believers. There was no church close to them, but when they could, they'd show up in Nonoai to attend church, but it wasn't often the whole family could attend.

It was not until we began going to their house for services that we understood the hardship it had been for them to travel to Nonoai. They had to cross the river in a leaky dugout canoe. Once on the other side of the river, they would walk four kilometers into town. At least we could drive down the steep, narrow road till we reached the river, though we had to cross the same way they did: in a leaky dugout canoe, with someone baling water while someone else rowed to the other side. On the bright side, we are happy to say that, despite all their hardships and travel hazards, one of Pedro and Isaltina Ferreira's sons is a pastor today, as are the sons of two other Christian families in that vicinity. One of them has a ministry with fishermen along the coast of the Atlantic Ocean in the States of Parana and São Paulo.

Pedro Ferreira's nine-year-old niece, Almirinda, was involved in an accident at Christmas time while putting sugar cane stalks through the wooden cylinder press. Somehow, her hand got caught in the press and was crushed. Her family lived near Ferreira's on the mountain side of the Passo Fundo River. Her father brought her into town and took her to the hospital in Nonoai for medical attention, facing hours of difficult travel to get there. By the time they arrived, the doctor had no choice but to amputate the hand at the wrist. She would be hospitalized for a while, and would not be able to go home for three weeks. Her father was poor, and depended on his sugar cane crop to support his family. He could not stay in Nonoai, but had to return home as soon as possible to produce the molasses and cakes of sugar that he could sell for his family's livelihood. He would also have to tend to his livestock.

Our friend Pedro Ferreira let us know about what had happened to his little niece and we assured him that we would take care of her. We told Almirinda's father that we would visit his little daughter in the hospital, and then, bring her to our home until she recovered. He set out for home, much relieved.

We knew that the father had no extra money to leave for her care, so, we let the doctor know he could use whatever antibiotics and other medication necessary, and we would pay for it. The doctor took us at our word: changing bandages regularly and applying medications, she received the best of care.

Nine-year-old Almirinda was such a trooper. Not once did she complain during the three weeks she was in our house. It was plain to see that she wanted to help wherever she could, and one-handedly, she would sweep floors and wash dishes. Helping Almirinda was a chance for us to leave a good testimony with her family, who were not Christians, and to sow gospel seed in the heart of our sweet little guest.

CHAPTER SIXTEEN

VISITORS FROM HOME AND POLITICS

You never grow too old or live too far away to wish you could share with your folks something that is happening! 1967 was the fulfillment of that wish for me! When we got the word that my parents, Granville and Marguerite Cothron, were planning to visit us, we were elated. And they were not coming for a 'pop-in kind of visit,' they planned to stay four weeks!

Ebba and I drove to Porto Alegre to meet them at the airport. After picking them up, we stayed in a hotel for the night, so they would be rested for the all-day trip the following day. The next morning we took off for Nonoai. When we reached the city of Passo Fundo, missionary friends invited us to dinner, a nice break, since we still had one-hundred miles to go.

It had rained, and the dirt road, which had recently been graded, was muddier than ever! Uphill and downhill we went, using four-wheel drive most of the time. At one point my father said, "I haven't seen this much mud since the First World War when I was in France!"

After five more hours of battling rain and mud, we arrived home. It was just after midnight when we pulled up in front of our house and were surprised to see the lights still on! Arlene and Beatriz were waiting for us, too excited to sleep. Still deep in my memory is the scene when we walked in: everyone hugging and talking at once! What a joyful reunion!

I wanted to show my parents everything I could, and wondered if four weeks would be long enough! We visited the Kaingang Reservation, and my folks told me it was much different than how they had imagined it to be. I think they felt more at home in the churches we visited, except that the messages were all in Portuguese! We made sure they had a taste of all the kinds of foods that would be new to them: some they liked, others not so much! They visited the school our kids attended, and marveled that our children felt so at home in a language so different from English!

They covered a lot of ground in those four weeks! For a couple already in their seventies, they held up well. My father even went with me to the hard-to-reach church down near the Uruguay River, and helped paint the inside of the church building.

One day, my dad, Derly, and I were walking down the street in Nonoai when a man came up to us and said, "You three look so much alike, the only difference is age and size." Kids and young people were drawn to my father. He would walk down the road with his arms around them while singing some little military ditty from years gone by in a language, of course, they could not understand, which made it even more entertaining for them!

The day came, oh too quickly, for them to leave us and return to the United States. We had received news that three more visitors would be coming, also from the United States, on the same day my folks were to travel! What to do?

"Do you think you could manage a bus ride to Porto Alegre on your own?" I asked them. They were game, so that was the plan!

I'm sure, however, both they and I were a little apprehensive when I put them on the bus. I had a little talk with the driver that went something like this: "Will you check on my elderly parents during the trip? They can't speak Portuguese." He assured me he would. I gave my dad a letter in Portuguese to use when they got to the airport to make sure they would get on the Varig Airline flight to the United States. And I gave them another note in English with instructions of what to do when they reached Porto Alegre. John Silk and his wife, missionary friends of ours, would be picking them up from the bus station and keeping them overnight.

There was no trouble with catching the flight—all went according to plan!

After my parents left on the bus, I took off for the city of Xapeco, Santa Catarina, forty miles away, to pick up our next visitors: Pastor Sherman Miller, Donald Slife (my brother-in-law), and Richard Peterson. They were on a month-long tour in South America, visiting missionaries who were sent out from the Englewood First Christian Church. (Later renamed Englewood Bible Church, but is no longer in existence.)

The men stayed a week with Ebba and me. We wanted them to comprehend the dual ministry we had, so we spent part of the time visiting Brazilian Christians in and around Nonoai, and the other part we spent on the Kaingang Reservation.

As we were hiking around the reservation, Pastor Sherman, who was known for his ready sense of humor, commented: "The Lord sure knew who to send to this place! It's only fit for mountain goats!"

"Are you calling me a *mountain goat?*" I asked, feigning indignation! And we all laughed as good friends do when poking fun.

April of 1967 was a great month for our family, and hopefully it opened the eyes of our visitors, and helped them to see firsthand some of the *fields that are white unto harvest.* My home church always promoted missions, which is probably why so many of the young people of the church, me included, have gone to mission fields across the world.

The overseas branches of New Tribes Mission (Ethnos360 since 2017) have always tried to replicate the same kind of training that missionary candidates receive in the United States. By 1967-68, the preliminary phase of training existed in Brazil, which was a Bible School, and now, they were ready to start phase two, which in the U.S. we referred to as *Boot Camp*.

Two or three locations were checked out. The one chosen had to do with its being remote and somewhat primitive. Clayton Templeton had become friendly with a medical doctor who was a Christian, and when Clayton explained what the mission was looking for, he offered his property in the State of Mato Grosso do Sul. "It is part of the large ranch I own, but I have no plans to ever use the most remote part as a ranch," he told Clayton.

When Clayton checked it out, it was just what we had been looking for: far enough from *civilization* to simulate areas where future Brazilian missionaries might someday be located. By April of 1968 the Brazilian *Boot Camp* training had begun!

Floyd and Ida Gilbert, and Stan and Dyann Donmoyer, who headed up the training, moved into an old farmhouse just off the property, and the students moved into houses made of sun-dried bricks and grass roofs. Typical of missionary students in training, the students were soon engaged in building a dormitory for new students. This construction had wooden sides and clay roof tiles.

Our Field Committee, of which I was a member, was scheduled to meet in April at this second phase training facility, which was called *Shekinah*. Ebba and I made the trip from Nonoai to Shekinah in our Jeep station wagon. We were gone for a couple of weeks. It took two days to get there: slow-going because there were few paved roads. I took the back seat out of the jeep before leaving Nonoai, and made a bed in its place for sleeping.

Once we arrived at Shekinah, I parked under the shade of a large mango tree. The days were warm, but nights were quite cool. Ebba and I slept very comfortably, but the other committee members, Abe Koop, Phil Davis, and Luiz Monteiro da Cruz, complained of being cold. I told them, "You need a *blanket with ears* like I have! I wasn't cold at all!"

I got some very strange looks! It took them a while to understand that I meant Ebba! Cuddling with her at night, close to her ears, kept me warm. I told them, "You should have brought your wives, too!"

Backtracking, I'd like to explain the affect politics have on missionaries, and on us during the 1960s. Politics in Brazil are always a hot item. That is why as foreigners, we missionaries take extra precautions to not get involved with, nor take sides in, any political campaign that might be in progress.

Brazil's Vice President, João Goulart, the Governor of the State of Rio Grande do Sul, Leonel Brisola, and the Mayor of Nonoai, Jair Calixto, were relatives. They all held strong far-left socialist political positions. Some very radical attitudes and actions by the Mayor of Nonoai and the Governor of our state, made life a bit scary and uncertain for everyone. Ebba and I were concerned about what might happen to our children in the future. The resignation of Janio Quadros, the country's President, in August of 1961 only added to the general unrest. The Vice President, João Goulart took over the Presidency at this time.

Ebba and I found ourselves threatened by the Mayor of Nonoai. He did not like Americans, and accused me of being a spy for the CIA. Armed men came to our house and took our Jeep. It was used in their revolutionary activities for almost a week. Someone remembered I owned a 22-caliber rifle, and that was also taken.

We became house prisoners, which meant we could not go anywhere away from town. We were not harmed, but the high tension that existed among the political rivals in town was very frightening. We'd be awakened at night by gunshots!

All the confiscated items were returned eventually. I decided to sell my gun, and buy a bicycle for Arlene with the money! Not having a gun, I reasoned, might help to prevent accusations of being a CIA agent! The American Consulate in Porto Alegre sent a man to check on our welfare. He stayed with us for a few days.

Finally, on March 31, 1964, the socialist element in Brazil was overthrown by the Brazilian Military, which was more conservative and democratic in philosophy. It ruled for nearly twenty-five years.

CHAPTER SEVENTEEN

TIME TO MOVE

We were mid-way in our year of furlough in the United States in the fall of 1971 when *the letter* arrived. There's something about receiving letters from headquarters! The return address on this one began *East Brazil Field Committee.* "Oh, my, what's wrong now?" I wondered before opening it to find out. I unfolded the pages, and skimmed through the first paragraph which was mostly greetings, and then, I read: 'Would you and Ebba accept a transfer from Nonoai to the Peniel Bible Institute?'

This was not the first time we had been approached about such a move, but up till this point we had not felt it was time to leave our work in Nonoai, not until there were others to replace us and more workers integrated into the work in southern Brazil. But now, other missionaries were fitting into the work in these areas. So, after some days of prayer and waiting on the Lord, we had peace in our hearts to say 'yes' to the proposed move.

We returned to Brazil in December of 1971, and stopped by Peniel for a quick look at where we would be living and working before continuing our journey by bus to Nonoai. Ebba and I were very familiar with the Bible Institute, which was in the south part of the state of Minas Gerais.

On many occasions we had gone there for Field Counsel meetings and Field Conferences, and since the founding of the Bible School in 1956, I had often been asked to speak in classes and for chapels.

We talked a lot on the bus as we headed home: HOME? It was hard to think about pulling up roots so deeply planted in Nonoai and in the Kaingang work, but we had only one month to make the move before classes would begin in Peniel, so we set to work sorting our things as soon as we arrived in Nonoai.

Some things were disposed of, other things we left in our house for missionary colleagues. When we sold our cow, it was almost like leaving a member of the family behind. Most of our belongings were loaded on a truck to be taken to the city of Erechim, where another trucking company would take them to São Paulo. And from São Paulo a trucker from the city of Jacutinga would bring our things to Peniel.

After our barrels, trunks, boxes, and furniture were loaded and gone, our family took a bus to São Paulo and then to Peniel.

While all this sounds cut and dried, there was a lot of work and emotions involved. Saying goodbye to our long-time friends in Nonoai, and other places in the state of Rio Grande do Sul was very difficult, especially for Arlene, Beatriz, and Derly! Changing schools is difficult for children, and ours were no exception. It helped to know that when we got to Peniel, there were going to be people we knew and loved. We would be working with Floyd and Ida Gilbert, and Calvin and Gwen Taylor, and with some of the Brazilian missionaries that we knew, Paulo and Neli Jancitski and Silvio and Penha Monteiro. We never dreamed at the time that one day, the Jancitskis' daughter, Priscila, would become our daughter-in-law, married to our son Derly.

We were given the choice of two places to live. One house had recently been remodeled and painted. It was located on the main street of Peniel opposite the dining hall. The other was a fixer-upper, located in what was called the upper village, and was more secluded. Much to everyone's surprise, we chose the fixer-upper. "I like the location of this house much more," Ebba confided, "can you imagine the traffic we would have had on the main street: everyone coming and going from the dining hall?"

I told her I agreed, and added, smiling, "The climb up and down the hill to the chapel, classrooms, and school office will keep me in shape!"

I painted the house and fixed what needed fixing before and after we moved in. The next year, we had a detached garage built with an office and a second bathroom and shower at the back. The extra bathroom was very helpful when we had company, which was often, and the office provided a quiet place to study and prepare for classes. It was a very pretty location, shaded by hundreds of tall, stately eucalyptus trees.

About the time we arrived at Peniel, one of the teachers was leaving and needed a home for her dog. And that is how we acquired a new member of the family, a jet-black spaniel dog that we named Timmy. He was a great pet, and followed me everywhere. When I was working in the Institute office, Timmy was always there with me, lying at my feet. At night, to save his reputation, we kept him on a long leash on the back porch of our house so he could not be accused of getting into the neighbor's garbage cans.

One day, Timmy got mixed up with a porcupine and came home with his face full of quills. Our kids wrapped Timmy in a blanket so they could hold him down while I pulled out the stubborn quills, one by one! Timmy howled something terrible. He had two more encounters with porcupines, but he was more experienced, so I didn't have so many quills to extract!

I was given three subjects to teach that first semester and that was considered a full load. Ebba helped in the finance department, and was also one of the counselors for girl students. One semester, she had fifty-nine girls to counsel. She set up a schedule so she could meet regularly with each one. She had things well organized, and managed our home and her jobs at the Institute with the same efficiency.

After only four months at Peniel Ebba came down with hepatitis for the second time: the first, when she'd been less than a year in Brazil. Bed rest is the only cure, and for several weeks her jobs were done by others while she kept to her bed. We took precautionary measures at our house so none of the rest of us became ill.

The schedule of a typical day at the Peniel Bible Institute went like this: chapel at 7:00 a.m., followed by breakfast. Classes were from 8:35 until 12:05. Lunch was followed by work detail, from 1:00 till 4:00. Weather permitting, sports such as volleyball or soccer were played until 5:00. Dinner was at 5:30, and from 7:00 till 10:00, study hall, after which students were to be in their dorms. Other activities took place on designated days, such as choir and counseling appointments.

On Sundays, all students were engaged in evangelism! They would be found in nearby towns, cities, and farmlands. Some had their own vehicles, others took buses, while still others walked as much as ten or twelve miles round trip. Sometimes teams were formed, made up of staff members and students, and they would visit churches in cities near and far to present the work of the Brazilian branch of New Tribes Mission and to challenge church members to become involved in mission endeavors.

Part of the practical evangelism training we offered students at Peniel were opportunities to work in churches. I would visit the church ahead of time to talk with the pastor, and arrange for students to gain experience by assisting him in the church. Then, I would match students to pastors and church needs.

On one such trip, Ebba and I went to the city of *'Espirito Santo do Pinhal'* (yes, I know that is a mouthful). This city was fifteen miles from the Institute. I wanted to check out the possibility of placing a student for weekend ministry in a small Baptist church there. I was told to confer with Dona Marieta, but the person who told me this didn't give me an address. Knowing nothing more than the name of the city where she resided, Ebba and I took off to try to locate Dona Marieta. Arriving, I asked some men on a street corner if they could tell me where Dona Marieta lived. I perceived she was well known because they promptly gave us directions to her house. As we parked, we saw lots of people, some on the porch, and some going in or out the front door. We wondered if Dona Marieta had died and there had been a funeral.

Hesitantly, I went to the door and asked for Dona Marieta. Far from being a funeral, we were told it was a birthday party for one of her great-grandsons. Marieta, a spry, hundred-year-old black woman, oversaw the whole affair. She made us feel at home and served us cake! She looked me over and said to Ebba, "He's too thin. You need to treat him better!"

That night we attended the little church which was located just across the street. Dona Marieta was still able to read the Bible in public without the aid of glasses! What a time we had that evening. As I recall, we did send a student to help this little congregation on weekends.

Two big mission conferences were held each year at Peniel, which were three-or four-day events. We always had a big turnout for the one held in February during Carnaval time. Church groups desired to come to Peniel for the mission conference to get away from the wild Carnaval orgies in their cities. The other conference was held at the close of May, when the first semester ended. The Institute usually hosted up to one hundred extra people when these conferences took place.

A third big event each year, at the beginning of December, was graduation. Although most people came just for the day, we generally had more than two hundred visitors. Sometimes whole busloads of people would come to attend the graduation ceremonies for students from their churches. Most of the visitors were parents, friends, and pastors.

As mundane as it might seem, if you were to look in on our times of prayer on the days leading up to graduation, you would hear *'Lord, please hold back the rain till graduation is over!'* Rain is frequent in December, and the tile roof on the chapel was famous for leaking, despite our many attempts to remedy the situation.

To coordinate their programs, the staff of the two mission institutes would meet annually for three days. Since I'd been on staff at Peniel, I also joined these planning sessions. On one occasion, it was held in Mato Grosso do Sul at the Shekinah Missionary Institute. As was generally the case, one of the subjects dealt with was the placing of staff members at the institutes. We were always short-handed, which involved shifting personnel from one campus to the other. John Enns, who was President of Peniel at the time, volunteered to move to Shekinah for one year because of an urgent need there. Though I did not feel adequate for it, I accepted when I was asked to take over the Presidency of Peniel in his absence, thinking that in a year John would return to Peniel.

The truth is, John Enns never did return, and I was President of Peniel for the rest of the time we were there. Later, I added to my responsibilities as President, those of the Academic Dean, since the man who held that position was due for a year's furlough with his family in the United States. It was almost too much for me, and we vowed to think ahead, and to never again be so short of teachers and Institute leadership that anyone would have to fill two positions. We had learned the reality of the adage, *'You can't spread yourself too thin and still do the job right.'*

Our work at the Institute was not easy: we were "on duty" twenty-four hours a day, including weekends, but it was rewarding! We spent ten years at Peniel, and when we began seeing former students serving as missionaries to indigenous tribes, and some in leadership positions in the mission, and still others pastoring churches, we knew our hard work had paid off!

Not every student was a success story, however. We were always quick to work with those students who failed, humbly admitted it, and had a desire to change, but others had to be dismissed. Some were unrepentant, and their influence on others endangered the morale of the student body. These were sad moments for all of us, and we prayed for each one who left school under those conditions.

We continue to praise the Lord for those who finished well, and are faithfully serving the Lord today. We smile whenever we hear about former students who are now on staff at the mission's Institutes! Who would know better how to motivate students than those who have been students themselves?

While we were on furlough in 1971, Arlene, our oldest daughter, graduated from South Denver High School, and began nurses' training. When the time came for the rest of the family to go back to Brazil, however, Arlene made the decision to return with us, and take the three-year Bible course at Peniel Bible Institute. It was a good decision; she graduated from Peniel in 1974.

When we became staff at Peniel, our daughter Beatriz and son Derly attended school in the nearby city of Jacutinga. I drove them, along with six or seven other kids, to school every morning at seven o'clock. School was over for them at noon—when I was the busiest at the Institute. A friendly farmer who would be picking up his own children, agreed to pick up the kids I had taken in the morning and deliver them to the Institute. We developed a lasting friendship with the farmer, Senhor Tete, and his wife, Dona Antonia. It was several years before this couple would allow us to speak about biblical matters and salvation, however.

Beatriz was showing real interest in piano while we were still in Nonoai, and had continued lessons with a piano teacher in Jacutinga. One day the teacher told me, "Beatriz is becoming so advanced, there is not much more that I can teach her." She referred us to another teacher in the city of Ouro Fino. Before long, however, that teacher let us know that Beatriz was ready for the Musical Conservatory in the city of Pouso Alegre. I had managed the drive back and forth to Ouro Fino, fourteen miles from Peniel, but the conservatory was fifty miles away, over curving, mountainous roads. Because it was important to my daughter, we made the trip once every week. While Beatriz was in classes for three or four hours, I would sit in the car under a streetlight, close to the Conservatory, and prepare for the next day's classes, or correct papers and tests. Most of the time, Beatriz and I didn't get home until 10:30 or 11:00 at night. We did this for a couple of years.

Beatriz came to the United States in mid-1976, and enrolled in Tennessee Temple University. There she met her husband-to-be, Daniel L. Steinman. They were married in 1981 in Norfolk, VA. At the time of this writing, Dan is Pastor of Freedom Baptist Church of Chesapeake, a church with a strong mission emphasis.

As I've mentioned before, it seemed best to us that our children receive both English and Portuguese schooling. We're happy to say, that as confusing as that seemed at times, weaving in year-long furloughs in the United States with our main residency in Brazil, our children managed to qualify for graduations in both countries. During our furlough in 1976, Derly completed his senior year and graduated from Englewood High School, my alma mater. But when we returned to Brazil, Derly still had some of the Brazilian school system requirements to meet, called *Ginásio* before he could graduate. He completed these in Jacutinga, and afterwards registered as a student at Peniel, where we were on staff, for the next three years. That gave us the privilege of having him with us just a little longer! He graduated from Peniel Bible Institute prior to attending and graduating from Tennessee Temple University.

We used the correspondence course offered by American School of Chicago for our children's English studies, and looking back we are so grateful that, although it took extra work for them and for us, our children have well-rounded educations in both English and Portuguese.

CHAPTER EIGHTEEN

VISITS, VACATION, AND A WEDDING

*O*ur family left Peniel early to attend the 1973 East Brazil Field Conference that would be held in Vianopolis. Ebba and I decided to go early so that, along the way, we could visit some people and places we hadn't seen or visited for a long, long time.

Our first stop was in the capital city of Brasilia, where we spent a night with Dr. José Peixoto da Silveira and Dona Galiana. They had been like parents to Ebba that first year in Brazil, and we had not seen them since our wedding. Dr. Silveira took us and our kids all over the city and showed us the tourist attractions and government buildings. He had been involved in the planning of the city from the time it was still ranch-land. He gave me an autographed book he had written about how the city of Brasilia came to be. We stayed in their home, and they treated us like family!

When we said goodbye to the da Silveira's, we left for Crixas. Yes, it had been twenty-one years since I left Crixas to get married! We were going to the place where I cut my teeth on speaking Portuguese, and I had no idea what we would find when we got there, but was anxious for Ebba and my children to see it. There was a paved highway as far as Ceres, but dirt roads from there on to Itapaci and Crixas: it was very dusty at this time of year. I explained to Ebba and the kids, "During rainy season, though, it's a sea of mud!"

We spent the night in a small hotel in Itapaci. I asked about people I had known in Crixas, and if they still lived there. We left Itapaci early the next day, and stopped along the road to make and eat our breakfast. Besides the dust, the road to Crixas resembled a washboard. To cross the creeks and rivers along the way, we had to drive on log bridges, being careful to line up the wheels of the car with the logs. All went well, praise the Lord, but it was a bit nerve-wracking! Close to noon, we drove into Crixas.

I asked a man where João Dietz lived, and he directed me to his house. I stood at the door of the house, and when I knocked, João himself answered. He stood looking at me, and finally said, "I should know you, but I can't remember your name."

Just then, his wife joined him at the door, and immediately called me by name. From that moment on, it is hard to describe all that happened. Word spread rapidly that we were in town, and people came from all over, among them the pastor-evangelist of the small Presbyterian Church in town. He asked if I would speak that night if he announced a meeting. I said I would be happy to preach.

During the afternoon we walked around the town that had become a city. I took Ebba to the house where I had lived in 1952 and showed her and the children the room I stayed in, the river where I washed my clothes and where Joel, and later Jack and I had our prayer meetings while our clothes dried.

That night we went to the Presbyterian Church, which was located on a hill, close to the jail and the Roman Catholic Church. I preached and gave an invitation. A man named Antonio came forward for salvation, and when he was walking down the aisle, an elder of the church joined him, a tender gesture I thought. The elder turned out to be Joaquim Dietz, the son of Pedro Dietz. Joaquim's wife was the first person I let to Christ during the early days of my ministry in Crixas.

I learned that Antonio, the man who was saved that first night, was the son of *Oscar*, the blacksmith who had guided Joel and me back to civilization, risking our lives while crossing dangerous rivers to get there! What a night of rejoicing: that God had chosen me to be the one to lead Oscar's son to the Lord, and to see Joaquim Dietz serving in the church! My cup was full to overflowing!

We'd have liked to have stayed longer in Crixas, but due to the dates of the Field Conference, we had to leave the next morning, amid the protests of the people in town. The Christians gave us oranges, cookies, and other Brazilian specialties to eat on our way. For the return trip to Ceres and then on to Vianopolis from there, we went through Rubiataba. (Joel and I had taken this route twenty years earlier by horseback to get to Crixas.) About twelve kilometers out of town we stopped for a short visit at a farm where one of the Christian families lived. Our children commented later that they had never seen such hospitality as we were shown in Crixas.

During the trip from Crixas to Rubiataba, God, once again, proved His faithfulness! As I shifted down, going around a curve and up a hill, an iron pin, like a small bolt, fell out of the shifting mechanism of our vehicle. Of course, I had to stop. I crawled under the car, and soon saw what the problem was. I thought, if I could find a piece of very heavy wire, I could do a temporary repair. I walked the road looking for what I needed, and within a hundred yards of the car, I found one of the spools on which some of the excess barbed wire had been rolled, when installing the barbed wire fence at the sides of the road. I cut a piece of wire, just the right size, and fixed the shifting lever, and we were soon on our way. The repair was not perfect, but it worked.

It would be another twenty-three years before Crixas came into the picture again (and that story I'll tell later).

We made it to Vianopolis for the Field Conference, and had just returned to Peniel when word came that Dona Maria, João Dietz's wife, had died, and that João was heartbroken. We were saddened as well, but so glad we had been able to see her before God took her home.

In December of 1974, after the semester ended and graduation was already history, Ebba and I decided it was time for a family vacation!

We asked our kids, "Which would you like for Christmas this year: presents or a family vacation?"

"A vacation!" they exclaimed!

It didn't take us long to throw things into our bags! We took hammocks, food, and a camping stove, jumped into our little yellow Ford station wagon, and took off.

But first things first! We headed for the city of Pirassununga so Ebba could have some dental work done. That taken care of, when evening came, we went off the highway about half a mile to a small park where we found a historical monument that honored soldiers from the Brazilian-Paraguayan War. There was a big tree right in the middle of the park where we could hang our hammocks. Other than a short-lived sprinkle of rain just before midnight, and a bat that Ebba and Beatriz said they saw, we had a peaceful night.

Our journey the next day took us across Goias into Mato Grosso where we stayed a night in Barra do Garças, the small town where Ebba and I had spent our honeymoon many years before. We also visited one of our former students who lived there, and attended her church that evening.

From there, we traveled north on a dirt road to the newly founded towns of Xavantina and Nova Brasilia where Gercino and Jucira Marques, former students from Peniel, were getting started in a new church planting ministry. We stayed with them for three days. Their house had only three rooms. To sleep, our hammocks had to be hung one above another—it was very hot and not exactly comfortable in such cramped quarters.

Though they had support for the ministry, it had not arrived yet, and they had nothing to feed us. We gave them money to buy some supplies, and they felt God had sent us to visit them *for such a time as this.*

While we were there, a group of Xavante tribal people came into the town. The Xavante are strong, tall people with black shoulder length hair and piercing eyes. The townspeople were afraid of them and told us, "Sometimes when they come into town, they'll walk into your house and take food right out of the pans on the stove if they are hungry."

We were somewhat uneasy ourselves at the time. But since then, the Xavante have been contacted and given the gospel. Today, there are many Christians among the tribe. Praise the Lord!

We left Gercino and Jucira, and retraced our steps back to the state of Goias. We took the road that led us to the historic city of Goias, once the capital of the state. On this leg of the trip, we found a very pretty place to camp alongside a nice creek hidden by trees. We fixed our supper and hung our hammocks once again. All was well until it began to rain! We took our hammocks down, and sat in the car. The rain was persistent, and it didn't look like it was going to stop, so we left our camping spot at 3:00 AM, and drove twenty kilometers into town! We got two small rooms in what our kids called a spooky, old hotel. The next day, after a good breakfast, we drove around town, visiting some of the historical sites, such as an old prison with stone walls nearly two feet thick, and several old Roman Catholic churches. Passing one house, Beatriz excitedly exclaimed, "Look, there's a man reading a Bible!"

I stopped the car, and went up to the porch of his house to speak to him. "Hello, is that a Bible you are reading?" I asked. He was quick to tell me it was and that he was a believer. After a brief chat, he directed us to the house where a Scottish missionary had lived years before when he traveled all over that part of the country on horseback, evangelizing. I had heard about this old Scottish missionary many times, and without ever having met him, I had, and have, a holy respect for him. Reminiscent of Steve's Green's lyrics:

Oh, may all who come behind us find us faithful,
May the fire of our devotion light their way.
May the footprints that we leave lead them to believe,
And the lives we live inspire them to obey.

Our kids say they will always remember this trip. There were funny things that happened, many serious events, and times that we will all remember forever. God was good to us.

By the late 1970's, Arlene had finished all her missionary training in the United States and was back in Brazil as a missionary, working in Vianopolis at our mission headquarters.

Arlene and Gil Baxter, a schoolteacher, took a trip during vacation time, and while passing through the city of Manaus, in the state of Amazonas, Arlene met a young man named David Johnson who was teaching in the school for missionary children. And the rest is history!

In December of 1979 David and Arlene were married in a beautiful outdoor ceremony in front of Floyd and Ida Gilbert's house, who lived near the Peniel Bible Institute. Our piano was loaded on Lyle Denelsbeck's pickup and taken to the wedding site. Except for the piano, all the other things needed were loaned by the Institute, benches from the chapel, and everything needed for the reception from the dining hall. Stan Donmoyer played the piano, and I performed the ceremony. David's mother and sister came from the United States for the wedding. David's mother had a difficult time understanding the popular Brazilian custom of cutting the groom's tie in pieces after the wedding. The scraps of the tie were sold, and the money collected was given to the newlyweds for their honeymoon trip! A lot of people cooperated to make Arlene and David's wedding the beautiful event it was, and we remain indebted to them.

CHAPTER NINETEEN

THE MOVE TO PERNAMBUCO

B y 1980, Peniel Bible Institute was running at almost full capacity. Many students were coming to us from Evangelical churches in northeast Brazil, which prompted the leadership of the Brazilian branch of NTM to start a second Bible School. The search for property in the northeast of Brazil was hardly begun when property was donated for that purpose. (Matthew 6:8, *"Your Father knows what you need before you ask him."*) The property was twenty-five miles outside Recife, the capital of the state of Pernambuco. Ebba and I were asked to go check it out.

In October, we traveled by bus to Recife where we were met by Sergio and Alda Scripnic, Brazilian national missionaries with NTM. They had moved onto the donated property to watch over it till something was decided. Sergio said, "We'll take you out to the property so you can look it over," and on the way he filled us in on what to expect.

"The property is comprised of thirty-seven acres of hilly land, and the land surrounding it, is used mainly for sugar cane. The owners operated an orphanage for a while, but closed it about six years ago, and wanted to donate both land and buildings to the mission to be used as a school for training Brazilians for missionary work. The buildings have been sitting empty and unused since then. It's really a mess, right now! Thousands of fruit bats and termites have taken over the buildings, and, for the most part, the wooden structures will all have to be replaced. Weeds and brush have grown up, making a good hiding place for snakes of all kinds, poisonous and otherwise. Things are in a sorry state, and though I've been plugging away at it, there's not much to show for it. I have gotten the water system operating properly, at least."

When we arrived, we were glad that Sergio had prepared us ahead of time, using the descriptors *mess* and *sorry state*, for that it was! We concluded there was potential, but it was going to require a lot of work and expense. The work on the existing buildings would include removing and moving walls, changing doorways, installing new plumbing and electrical wiring, and many other things. New buildings would be needed: classrooms, a dorm for single men, a dorm for single women, apartments for married couples. Furniture needed included tables, benches, bunk beds, desks, shelving. Hardly any of the furniture left in the buildings was fit to use. There was a nice-sized chapel, a dining room/kitchen area, and a large garage/shop combination, which only needed new roofing. There were many cashew and mango trees on the property. The five-kilometer dirt road from the future campus to the main highway was going to be a never-ending challenge in the rainy season.

Yes, we concluded, it was a valuable donation and a good place for a second Bible School, but it was to be understood that the rebuilding and maintenance would be ongoing even after it opened, and probably for many years. And that prophecy came true: the ten years we lived there, the rebuilding and renovating provided the "work detail assignments" for the students!

There was to be another furlough for us in the last part of 1981, before we took up residence in the *Macedonia Bible and Missionary*

Institute, as it was called. Soon, when speaking about it, the name was shortened to 'Macedonia.'

We returned to Peniel to retrieve the things we had left there while on furlough. We had stored all our furniture and other belongings in a small, unused house on the property. While we were gone, a limb from a nearby eucalyptus tree had fallen through the tile roof of the house, but went unnoticed. Rain had destroyed some of our things, including one mattress! We arranged for a truck from Jacutinga to take our things from Peniel, in the state of Minas Gerais, to Recife, in the state of Pernambuco, 1,800 miles away.

I talked over the cost for such a long trip with the trucker. One look at my face as he pronounced the sum, alerted him to the fact that it was considerably more than I had anticipated. He was quick with a solution, "A tile company has asked me to take a ton of tile to Recife. Why don't I combine that order with yours? That would reduce the cost for you." Much relieved, I agreed to it, and he said he'd be coming by the Institute in the morning to pick up our things.

With the help of staff and students, we loaded all our furniture, boxes and barrels on the truck and covered the whole load with a huge canvas. The next morning, at 4:00 a.m., Ebba and I met the trucker on the highway at the entrance to Peniel. For the next four days, we rode in the cab of the big Mercedes truck with the driver.

The first two days of the journey took us through the Mantiqueira Mountain Range. The truck crawled up the steep grades in first and second gear. Around 10:00 each night, he'd stop at a simple hotel, and we would sleep for a few hours. But we'd take off at 5 the next morning for the next leg of the journey. Brazilian truck drivers are famous for putting their trucks in neutral on downgrades, supposedly to save fuel, and our driver was no exception. He loved to tell us stories about some of his friends whose brakes had failed when trying to save fuel, and how they'd gone over the bank and been killed!

As Ebba watched the speedometer reach sixty miles an hour going down some of the hills, she hung on to me for dear life, hoping the brakes wouldn't fail! During the last day or two, our driver became very sleepy. Ebba would whisper to me, "Talk to him, Alton, so he won't go to sleep!" On the last day, he finally pulled over and slept for a little while, and Ebba and I got out and sat alongside the road to give him more room while he slept.

It was night when we left the main highway out of Recife and pulled into a gas station where the five-kilometer dirt road started that led to the soon to open Macedonia Bible and Missionary Institute. Because the road would be difficult for a heavily loaded truck to navigate after dark, the driver stayed with the truck at the gas station. Ebba and I hired a local man to take us the rest of the way. We were warmly greeted by our colleagues. Gerson and Maria Theresa Celete served us tea and crackers, and got a bed ready for us in the apartment above them where we would live for the next ten years. But as we went into our apartment, the stench from bat manure and urine was horrible! We tried to remedy the situation, but the stench remained even after removing bat droppings *by shovelfuls*. Finally, overcome with tiredness, we slept.

The next morning, Lyle Denelsbeck and I drove to the gas station to lead the way back to Macedonia for the truck. There was one hill so steep that the driver had to make two attempts to reach the top because of the heavy load. Once we arrived at our destination, trailed by the truck, it took several hours and several men to unload everything.

Ebba and I began the big job of cleaning up the apartment that was to be our home: task number one, getting rid of the bats! Then came painting, putting in a kitchen sink, and mounting cupboards—all the things that needed doing before moving our furniture and household goods into the apartment. The improvements we made eventually included a bat-proof, cement ceiling, new windows, and a make-over of the bathroom.

We found the constant heat and humidity of northeastern Brazil hard to adjust to, especially for Ebba, who would say, "All I have to do is pick up the broom to be dripping in sweat." We had no need for a blanket or sweater for the ten years we lived there. Temperatures never go below 65 degrees, and the humidity is always high, even in the dry season. Despite our battle with bats and climate, we made many friends: people we could count on.

"A true friend will not only love when it is easy, but at all times."
(Proverbs 17:17- a simplified version).

For the first couple of months on staff in Macedonia, we did not have a car, but I kept my eye open for one that we could afford and found in Recife: a four door Chevy sedan at just the right price for my billfold.

The date set for the Inauguration Service for the *Instituto Bíblico e Missionário Macedônia* was January 30, 1982. Prior to that date, a lot of effort was put forth so that nothing would detract from the new institute's opening. Ed and Maggie Harper, who were dear friends and colleagues of ours, came from the interior of the state of Pernambuco to help. The four staff couples also rolled up their sleeves: there were Sergio and Alda Scripnic, Lyle and Louise Denelsbeck, Gerson and Maria Theresa Celeti, and Ebba and I. When the Elmbrook Church in Wisconsin heard about the inauguration, and how much work was yet to be done, a group of volunteers came to lend a hand for two weeks!

The date arrived, and so did the people! The chapel was filled with friends and pastors from Recife and other nearby cities; missionaries came, some from the Word of Life mission; Larry Minter, former director of the orphanage, came and must have been impressed with all the changes. The four young people who would be the first students to attend the institute took it all in! Paulo Carrenho, a veteran missionary, represented Peniel and was the guest speaker. The Macedonia Bible and Missionary Institute was now a reality!

The day after the inauguration ceremony, classes began, following very much the same scheduling and curriculum that we used at Peniel. Each new semester brought new students and within a year or so, there were close to twenty young people attending.

At the end of the first year, one of the girl students dropped out, but the other three original students continued, and are active missionaries today, working with indigenous people groups. Ronaldo da Cruz Lima married a student from Macedonia, and they worked for years with the Maxacali tribe in the eastern part of the state of Bahia. I had the privilege of performing their wedding in the city of Natal, in the state of Rio Grande do Norte. Sara Scripnic, married now, worked with the Yanomami tribe in northern Brazil with her husband. Silvana and her husband, who also attended Macedonia, work in the city of Manaus in western Brazil.

Because Macedonia had a much smaller enrollment than Peniel, there was a closer student/teacher relationship, and we could help our students in ways not always possible with a larger student body. Here we were more like a family.

To make the Brazilian Branch of NTM known in the northeast part of the country, where most had never heard of it, we began visiting churches and pastors. When invited to speak, we presented the challenge of becoming involved with reaching the unreached in Brazil. We left mission literature at each contact, and let it be known that we had Bible Institutes that prepared students for missions as well.

João Campos, a Brazilian pastor in Recife, had a TV program on a local station, and he interviewed Gerson Celeti and me a couple of times, which helped people in and around Recife to know about Macedonia and its mission to prepare students for missionary work among indigenous people groups.

We soon discovered our school was just one of several Bible institutes and seminaries in the area. The two largest were the Northern Baptist Seminary and the Presbyterian Seminary. It took some time and effort for us as a school and mission to become known and to gain credibility in such a context. Interestingly, one of the professors at the Presbyterian Seminary, by the name of Frans Leonard Schalkwijk, from Holland, had been challenged for missionary work many years before by Paul Fleming, the founder of New Tribes Mission. We became good friends with Frans Schalkwijk.

It was very good news for us when we learned that Conrad and Isabel Krieger would be coming for a two-month visit in 1982. The Kriegers and Cothrons attended the same church in Englewood, Colorado, and after I married, whenever we were on furloughs, Ebba and I always spent time with Con and Isy in their home. It was exciting for us to be entertaining them in ours! Conrad was a carpenter and the kind of man who saw what needed to be done. He just had to be busy! He had no sooner arrived than he was making kitchen cupboards, and items for the chapel and dormitories. Isabel helped organize our library and made herself useful in other ways, as well. They were a great blessing and loved by all. This couple had a heart for missions.

This wasn't their first visit, however. When we were on staff at the Peniel Bible Institute, they came with Paul and Betty Allen, also from the Englewood Church, to visit us.

As with any group of young people, our students liked to play pranks: and staff members were fair game! I had a bicycle that I was going to give to another missionary who worked in the small town of Porto Real do Colégio, in the state of Alagoas, some two hundred kilometers south of Recife on the north side of the mighty São Francisco River. Late one afternoon, I put the bicycle in the car after removing the front wheel, and locked the car. We intended to leave early the next morning to deliver the bicycle.

During the night, three of our students, not knowing I had already put the bike in the car, climbed up a ladder onto the second-story porch that ran full length along the back side of the building we lived in, where I had been keeping the bike. They planned to take the bicycle and hide it. When they discovered it was not on the porch, not to be foiled, they switched gears and decided to sneak into our living room, roll up our rug, and hide it instead!

Ebba awoke and said, "Alton, I heard something! Someone's in our house!"

I wasn't too happy about getting up, but finally did! I went to the living room, turned on the light and caught the three fellows red-handed, quietly moving furniture and rolling up the rug. As if they'd seen a ghost, all three ran out the door, down the porch, banging into the washing machine, and making a loud noise! They shimmied down the ladder, and disappeared into the night.

By this time, I was sitting on the floor, laughing my head off. Ebba ran to the living room, saw me on the floor, and thought I had been attacked. She was also afraid someone might have stolen the mission funds she had left on the table ready to distribute the next morning. Ebba was treasurer and handled the monthly mission allowances. Don and Dalvani Austin, who lived in the apartment below us, woke up with all the commotion and called, "What's going on up there?"

The three boys were scared and wondered what would happen to them, so they were relieved to see us laughing and taking it all in our stride! No punishment was meted out, and a good laugh was had by all. But we admonished them, "You'd better not pull this kind of prank again!"

A young married man enrolled in the institute who was blind. He was intelligent and his hearing had developed more than average: he could recognize who was coming just by the person's walk. Someone sent him a typewriter for Braille, and I helped him get it out of customs. Whenever I gave a test in class, I administered it separately for him. I would dictate the questions and he would write the answers on an ordinary typewriter so that I could read them. A lot of additional help was necessary for him, but his wife and other students were quick to provide it.

On the wild days of Carnaval a half million people can be found in the streets of Brazil dancing, singing, drinking, and parading, not to mention the immorality that went on! It was known that there were always Christian Conferences in Peniel during Carnaval, and Macedonia was flooded with requests from people who wanted to spend those three or four days away from the city. We accepted the number of people we felt we could accommodate, providing a mission conference with music, films, preaching, and literature. All afternoon people could participate in sports or just have fun cheering on the teams! We did our best, and prayed that the Lord would bring from the conference things of eternal value.

The escape we provided from Carnaval, was also a good advertisement for Macedonia.

We had other missionary conferences as well and invited church people in the area to attend them. One thing we did during a missionary conference that was very effective was the missionary hike through the woods. One or two of our men served as guides and took groups of visitors over the trail that had been prepared ahead of time. The objective was to give the visitor an idea of what tribal missionaries face as they attempt contact with an ethnic group to evangelize it. At one point, the visitors would come upon a staged Indian house with real "live" Indians, bows and arrows and other items menacingly on display.

We had many experiences during our years in Brazil, but one thing we experienced while living in the state of Pernambuco, tops them all! Ebba and I were robbed at gunpoint. We were on our way into the city of Recife, about 25 miles away. Coming from Macedonia, we pulled into the gas station from the dirt road to put fuel in our car.

There were several others fueling their vehicles, including a truck loaded with bananas. Ebba noticed the lady who owned the station and pointed her out to me: she was sitting on a tall stool and shaking like a leaf. We thought she was sick or having some sort of seizure. I got out of the car, and started for the pump, when a man came up to me and pulled a gun from under his shirt and pushed it into my stomach, saying, "This is a holdup and I want your money!" I had only a few cents in change, but he took that, and then took our watches. He tried to get my wedding band, but it wouldn't budge, and he gave up. (Later, when I wanted to joke about it, I commented, "We've been married so long, I guess my ring must have rusted to my finger!") We saw that this was just one of four men involved in robbing people, and that we weren't the only victims. Two of the robbers were standing close by us, armed, and keeping an eye on the victims, a fourth was in a stolen automobile, waiting as more people at the station were being held up. We heard the man in the car yell, "Let's go!" The accomplices ran for the car, and it sped off as soon as they were inside. No one had been hurt or killed, but we were all very shaken!

Ebba and I thanked the Lord for His protection. We were told the gas station had been robbed like that more than once. From that time on, we never drove into any gas station without first checking the surroundings.

There was a constant turnover of staff during the years we worked in Macedonia. Due to health problems, Lyle and Louise Denelsbeck returned to the United States after serving two years with us at the Institute. Gerson and Maria Theresa Celeti left us to prepare to go to India as missionaries, and though they never made it to India, the Lord led them to Africa, where they worked for many years.

God always provided others to fill the places left vacant. Some that joined us were still single: Valmir Brisola, João Batista Mendes, and Leila one of our former students, who later married.

Another couple, who were former students, who worked at the Instituto Macedonia with us for several years, was: Don and Dalvani Austin. Arlindo and Lelia Pereira were not former students of ours, and though they were more advanced in years, were still a good addition to our staff. Arlindo was a carpenter, and he was kept busy with his saw and hammer. Lelia was a good cook and oversaw the kitchen, but what she was most remembered for were her desserts, and how she shared them with anyone approaching the kitchen.

Other replacements that came to Macedonia included: Roque and Alba Camargo, José Marcos and Valeria Braga, and Joab and Roseli Ferreira. Joab oversaw maintenance and construction. (Joab and Roseli had worked with us in Peniel.)

In 1986, former students from Peniel, Marcos Tadeu Torres, and Zilma, whose last name I no longer remember, came to serve in Macedonia. And in 1987, Lowell and Thelma Denelsbeck joined our staff.

At one point all the staff at Macedonia had, at one time, been our students when we were working in Peniel. Ebba and I found this to be quite unique and a great privilege. As new staff members came, others left, some returning to tribal works, others entered ministries with churches.

Just a little over a half mile from the Macedonia Bible and Missionary Institute was the Word of Life Camp, and from the beginning, we had a close relationship. Word of Life students and staff were always invited to our activities such as meetings with special speakers, banquets, conferences, and other events. Word of Life did the same for us.

One of our staff was always invited to teach during their camp season, as well as at the one-year Bible School course that Word of Life offered. I taught a course on missions there, and Ebba spoke to girls and ladies' groups. Their students and our students competed in sports, mostly soccer. Over the years, all this interchange has resulted in several Word of Life students, upon finishing their studies at Word of Life, coming to Macedonia to continue missionary training. Some now work with NTM in Brazil.

Students and staff from both Macedonia, and Word of Life, joined to produce an hour-long cantata entitled "Love Story," and performed it over forty times in churches all over northeastern Brazil. It was a lot of work, and we practiced for months, but it was well worth the effort. Not only did it have a good, spiritual message, but it shined a light on the objectives of each school.

While we were still working in the Peniel Bible Institute, Ebba knew she had a large gall stone. The doctor who discovered it told her that if she was careful about what she ate, she could go many years without having any trouble. For over fifteen years she kept trouble at bay, but then, one Friday night, Ebba had a gallstone attack and was very sick. We managed to talk to the doctor in Recife by phone late that night, and he gave us some instructions to get her through the weekend. Monday morning, we went to see him, and within a few days Ebba was in the hospital for surgery. A Brazilian doctor, trained in the United States, removed the gall bladder and stone. Because the gall bladder was very inflamed, it turned out to be a difficult and delicate surgery, which took much longer than expected. But in the end, Ebba recovered very well. She received good care in the hospital in Recife, a fact which contradicted some of the wild tales we had heard about hospitals there.

During the years we worked in Macedonia in northeast Brazil, Arlene and David Johnson, our daughter and son-in-law, worked in the central part of the state of Maranhão, near the town of Barra do Corda, with the Canela tribe. We made one trip by car to visit them, and later another trip by bus, while our twin granddaughters were still tiny.

Quite a few of our students that have studied in Peniel or Macedonia are working with our mission today, either in tribal work or in some administrative capacity. We are so thankful to have had a part in their lives!

CHAPTER TWENTY

MOVE TO ANAPOLIS

The Macedonia Bible and Missionary Institute had been our residence and our work for nine years when we learned there was serious talk about our being transferred to the mission headquarters in Anapolis. We had already begun thinking that moving to a place with a more temperate climate would be better for Ebba's health: living in the state of Pernambuco had been hard on her since the day we first arrived. Ebba's health was a major factor in our acceptance of working in Anapolis.

Many of our moves have taken place after a furlough year, and the move to Anapolis, was no exception. When we returned to Brazil from our furlough in 1991, we went straight to Anapolis. We found a house to rent across the street from the mission office building. We located a trucker who was taking a load to Recife and contracted with him to bring our possessions from Macedonia to Anapolis. Ebba and I flew to Recife, and found Lowell Denelsbeck waiting at the airport to drive us to the Institute.

We started getting things ready for the truck, which arrived within a few days. The driver wasted no time, and as soon as our things were loaded, he took off for a four- or five-day trip back to Anapolis.

Ebba and I left a few days later in our car, after bidding our colleagues and friends farewell: something missionaries are never prepared to do. It's a bittersweet time. You don't want to repeat the usual clichés, *we're going to miss you,* etc., instead, you depend upon lingering hugs and firm handshakes to convey how you feel.

The first half of our three-day trip was uneventful, but the last half a different story! At the end of day one, we stayed with some Brazilian friends in the city of Feira de Santana in the State of Bahia.

The next day we continued our westward journey across the State of Bahia, but as we were nearing the town of Ibotirama, Ebba commented, "You know what, I haven't seen hardly any traffic coming from the opposite direction."

We found out the reason for this when we arrived in Ibotirama. The São Francisco River was flooding! Part of the town was under water and roads on the other side of the half-mile-long bridge were washed out. It was plain we wouldn't be continuing our journey, at least not that day, so we looked for a hotel that was not in the flooding area, and found a vacancy. Hotels were filling up fast, as you can imagine. To add to our joys, we did not have money to stay very long in a hotel. Something had to change, and soon!

"Maybe we ought to turn back, Ebba, and take another highway even though it would add quite a few extra miles to reach Anapolis," I suggested. But before making a rash decision, we prayed.

The following day, trucks were bringing in loads of huge rocks to fill in the washed-out bridgeheads. And dirt was being dumped on top of the rocks. We remained on the alert so that if the road opened, we would leave. And it did open, the second morning of our stay at the hotel. Crossing the repaired places was a bit scary. The highway we traveled on was more like a little ribbon in the middle of a brown ocean. It was only open for thirty or forty minutes before it was shut down again. We were one of the few cars to cross, before it closed.

Something Ebba ate at the hotel had not settled well! She became very sick and vomited. Here we were in the desolate, hot, interior of Bahia, miles from any kind of medical help! The sick feeling persisted, but somehow, she bore it for the next day and a half! Only God knows how! We still had to spend one more night on the road before arriving in Anapolis.

When we finally got there Ebba was feeling better: a good thing, because the truck had already unloaded our furniture, trunks, barrels, and boxes inside the house we would live in. Everything was covered with a heavy coat of dust. We had to wash all the furniture, and clothing, more than once. Within a few days, however, the house was in order, and I had reported to the office to learn my new job.

I had been a member of the East Brazil Field Counsel for many years, so part of my job, along with other members, was to meet and discuss plans, needs, lay strategies, help missionaries (counseling and encouraging them), and to make trips to tribal locations to give on-site spiritual and emotional help to the missionaries. The other part of my work was the never-ending Mission Correspondence, which I was to read and respond to whether written in English or Portuguese.

Ebba and I enjoyed trips to mission stations in our new, official capacity. When we arrived, we'd fit right in with the missionaries, and didn't have to be treated as tourists. Whatever the individual or team was facing, we understood: having *been there ourselves*. The many years working in Nonoai and on the Kaingang Reservation prepared us to listen to the missionaries in hard spots, and to come up we suggestions that were plausible. This type of ministry, we learned, helps reduce the drop-out rate of missionaries: being heard is powerful and a real help to people.

We made several long trips to visit missionaries in different parts of Brazil in 1992, accompanied by another Leadership Committee Member, José Cunha. We spent three to four days in each place. We visited the Shekinah Missionary Institute in Mato Grosso do Sul, and from there we traveled further south to Nonoai, in the state of Rio Grande do Sul. We found traveling as a couple on trips a good thing. Some of the things that a missionary wife faces are best dealt with by another woman.

We were only home for a few days after those trips, when we left Anapolis on another assignment, this time we headed north to the state of Maranhão to visit missionaries working in several tribal areas: the Timbira (later referred to as the Gavião), the Krinkati, the Krahô, and the Apinajé. José and his wife, Diva, went with us. Getting in and out of the Gavião and Apinajé tribes by vehicle was difficult because of the terrain, which was deep, loose sand. Our car kept bogging down in the sand, and we'd have to dig the tires out of the sand, or push them out to get through, and when we returned to Anapolis, we had an expensive car repair bill to pay. We praised the Lord for air conditioning all along the way through these remote areas, but it quit on us on our return trip to Anapolis.

Our appreciation for missionaries who face these kinds of hardships daily increased after that trip! Despite the sacrifice involved, they go on breaking down languages, and learning to speak clearly so they can give unreached people the gospel. These missionary teams, foreseeing the day they will give the tribe God's Word in their own language, make reading primers, and teach the people to read so they can read what God has to say in their own language! All the work is done by faith, that someday in the future, there will be a harvest!

It's a thrill for us today when we hear about good harvests in some of the tribes we visited, such as the Gavião and Krinkati where there are now groups of solid, growing Christians. The Krahô and Apinajé people, however, have been more resistant to the Gospel, but despite this, Bible teaching continues, and now there are some who believe. There are two main Apinajé villages and numerous smaller camps. We spent a few days in each of the main villages on our trip.

Ebba and I, and Jose and Diva took a third trip to the northeast of Brazil. Our tribal visits this time included the Kariri people near the town of Porto Real do Colégio, in the state of Alagoas, the Pancarurú and Pancareré near the city of Paulo Afonso, in the state of Bahia, and the Fulniô near the town of Águas Belas, in the state of Pernambuco.

Our former co-workers, Floyd and Ida Gilbert, pioneered the work among the Kariri. It has been difficult to plant churches in this tribe, however. The Kariri, and other tribal groups in the northeastern part of Brazil are highly integrated into Brazilian society as far as work and the mundane things of life. Though they have retained little or nothing of their native language, their culture is still very much in evidence, and that is what keeps them from integrating spiritually with Christians and churches in their communities.

Wherever we went on these trips, we found former students of ours, either from Peniel or Macedonia, working among the tribal people. This always brought much joy to our hearts. They were the fruit of our labors, and spiritual children that we were so proud to see all grown up in the Lord and serving him in hard places.

Throughout the years that I worked at the mission headquarters Ebba was free to pursue other avenues of service. Of course, she would have been willing to work at headquarters also, but being accessible to teach, speak, and show hospitality brought her much satisfaction.

There were quite a few Brazilian missionary candidates who would come to Anapolis on their way to work in other countries. Many of them wanted to learn English, and tapped Ebba to teach them. One couple, Jairo, and Vania de Oliveira, who went to Africa, have told us several times, that they have appreciated the English they learned from Ebba. Ebba also had a great ministry in hospitality. She was always quick to provide meals and lodging for people coming through Anapolis. Some stayed with us overnight, and others for days or weeks.

Rather than having Sunday worship at headquarters, it was decided that mission personnel would do well to take advantage of the different churches across the city, and we started our own search for a church. Some of our co-workers were going to a Presbyterian Church close by the mission. We attended a few times, but being a bit concerned about some of its practices, we continued to look. Other colleagues were attending a church, pastored by a Brazilian member of our Mission, and though it was a good church, after going a few times, Ebba and I decided to look for a church where none of the Mission personnel were in attendance.

We felt we were where God wanted us right away when we visited the First Baptist Church in downtown Anapolis. We became members, and friends with the Pastor, Geraldo Ventura da Silva. One day the pastor asked if we would consider helping one of the small congregations the church had started in the suburbs. We told him we would be happy to help, so one day he drove me to the suburb of Jaiara to meet the people from that congregation.

There were only a few people attending the services. One lady, in her sixties, was blind, diabetic, and on dialysis three times a week. The congregation consisted of that lady, her grown son, her sister, another young man, and a couple with two small children. Ebba and I worked with this group for three years. Sometimes, people from the mission would attend, among them, Stan, and Dyann Donmoyer. The group slowly grew in number and in the faith. Their building underwent some much-needed repairs and improvements, which made it more appealing to those who came to check it out.

When the blind lady, Dona Maria, died, I presided at her funeral. Not long after, an elderly man, who had been attending faithfully, was hit by a car, and killed while crossing a street. I also officiated at his funeral. The couple with the two small children did not have a car, so we would go by their house each Sunday morning and take them to church, and when church was over, take them home. We've heard that they are still active in the little church.

When Ebba and I left on furlough, another man from the main church downtown took over for us, and under his ministry, the church grew even more, and the facilities were upgraded quite a bit.

After furlough, Ebba and I became involved in the church downtown. Ebba participated in ladies' meetings, and did visitation. When a group of teens went on a retreat, Ebba was tapped to go along as a counselor. It wore her out, but she loved it and so did the teens. They invited her back the next year. I sang in a men's group and enjoyed that very much. Many different times I was invited to fill the pulpit for the pastor. We have fond memories of the people of the First Baptist Church of Anapolis.

One year, they gave me a surprise party on my birthday. Somehow, I learned about it ahead of time, so it wasn't really a surprise: but it surprised our neighbors! Fifty-eight people came that evening, with meat for a Brazilian barbeque, and each family brought food to go with it. A good time was had by all, and the party didn't end until two in the morning. The street was lined with cars and the neighbors must have wondered what was going on!

One Sunday, I was surprised! During the morning service Pastor Geraldo introduced several visitors. One was a lady by the name of Virginia who had come from Crixas, one of the first places I had gone as a missionary. While we were singing a hymn I went over to her, and quietly asked her if I could speak to her at the end of the service.

Later, when we talked and I told her my name, she said, "Oh, I'm so happy to meet you! I have heard about how you came to Crixas and evangelized our town long ago."

To my continuing surprise, Virginia returned to Anapolis a couple of weeks later with an invitation for me to speak at the twelfth anniversary of the Baptist Church in Crixas. Pastor Geraldo, I learned, was the one who had started the Baptist Church there. I was happy to accept the invitation. When the people from the Presbyterian Church in Crixas heard I was coming, they asked that I preach in their church, too! The date set was June 10, 1997.

The day arrived! We were returning to Crixas, in the state of Goias, with hearts full of expectations, but hardly prepared for all we would see, hear, and do during our visit! It took only four hours of travel to cover the same distance it had taken me nearly five days to cover forty-five years earlier. Automobiles and paved highways do make a big difference! We went from Anapolis to Ceres, then to Itapaci, as we had back then, but now the paved road took us through Pilar de Goias, an old historic town, and then to Santa Terezinha de Goias, which is a relatively new city, and finally, to Crixas.

It was next to impossible to recognize anything as far as the town of Crixas was concerned. It had grown so much and spread out over the surrounding hills, that were covered with brush and trees when I lived there.

It was late afternoon when we arrived, and we were directed to the home of Antonio and Sebastiana, where we would stay for the weekend. Their home was very large with many rooms, and was in the center of the city. They had prepared for our visit, and were awaiting our arrival.

Soon we had baths and a light lunch, after which we went to the Baptist Church for the first of four messages I would preach over the weekend. It was a joy to preach that night. There was a full moon which added a touch of charm to the evening. The church building was at the top of a hill from which we could see much of the city. After the service, Ebba and I went to the home of one of the church families for supper: a simple, abundant, and delightful supper served on the large porch at the back of the home. We didn't get to bed very early that night.

Our host, Senhor Antonio, took us into a little room just off their bedroom. In this little room was a chair, a small table with a Bible and a devotional book on it. He told us, "This is where my wife, Sebastiana, comes every day for a time of meditation and prayer." We could see why the gospel had made such strides in this town: prayer changes things! Sebastiana is a granddaughter to Dona Francisca, whom the people of the town had nicknamed *Vó Chica,* in whose house I had lived in the early days, preaching every night by lamplight in her living room.

The next day, Saturday, a great-granddaughter of Dona Francisca drove us four miles out of town to a huge, multinational gold mining operation. This lady's husband, who was an engineer at the mine, was an elder in the church. For over a hundred years, people had been panning gold in the Rio Vermelho (Red River) near town, but now modern technology has taken over. He took us by truck to a tunnel that spiraled down into the ground to a depth of four hundred yards. We went down the tunnel as far as the two-hundred-yard mark, where they were taking out ore. It was very impressive, to say the least.

We arrived back in town in time for a noon dinner with Antonio and Sebastiana. What a feast! And what fellowship! They had invited all their relatives who knew me in 1952. They had set up three tables, end to end, nearly twenty-five feet in length, to accommodate the guests. All had been saved except one lady, one of his sisters, who had remained a Roman Catholic. Lots of pictures were taken by different ones.

A beautiful thing happened Saturday evening at Presbyterian Church, also located on a hill at the head of the old town square. There were many descendants of the Dietz family attending the service who had been converted over the years. One of the elders of the church, came up to me and said: "Do you remember the baby you took in your arms in 1952 and dedicated to the Lord? Well, I am he!" He had become a very large man, and I was still a modest-sized preacher of God's Word. He smiled, looked down at me and asked, "Do you want to take me in your arms and rededicate me to the Lord?"

I looked up and said, "We can do it, but my prayer would have to be short." We laughed at the image of *me* taking *him* into my arms again. But I was rejoicing inside to see, in person, God's answer to my prayer of dedication!

Sunday morning found us back at the Baptist Church, which was full of people, some we had known years ago, and others, we were seeing for the first time. A man came up to me and told me he was Almerinda Pereira's brother. Almerinda was a missionary now with our mission, working with the Karaja tribal people, and her brother was proud of her. He was a faithful Christian himself and an active member of the church. (He has since died and gone to his heavenly home).

After the service, we went to visit some people who lived on the edge of town, and then to the home of a member of the church named Elias, where an anniversary dinner was being served, to celebrate the Baptist Church's twelfth anniversary! I am not sure of the number, but there were at least a hundred people participating. Once again, the meal was bountiful: rice, salads, barbeque and all the trimmings!

Sunday afternoon women from both the Baptist and Presbyterian churches gathered at the Baptist Church where Ebba had the honor of being their guest speaker.

Early Sunday evening, we were invited to the home of Antonio Leopoldino for supper, and that was very special for us. Antonio was the man who had gone forward to accept Christ during our family's visit to Crixas in 1973! His whole family had since come to know the Lord, and were attending a different church in town. We had a good meal and a wonderful time of fellowship.

And after supper, we headed for the Presbyterian Church for the final service. That service was impressive. Dona Sebastiana presented a history of the gospel in Crixas. The pastor asked those who were descendants of Vó Chica (Francisca) to stand up. At least ninety percent of the people stood. The scene was enough to bring tears to anyone's eyes. Truly the Gospel is the power of God unto salvation. Though Dona Francisca had died years before, her testimony and prayers have been influential over decades in bringing people to Christ.

Well, it was over, that wonderful weekend in Crixas! The next day, we headed back to Anapolis, but it took a long time for our hearts to absorb all that we had seen and heard while there.

The story does not really end at this point, however, because the following year we were invited back to preach again in Crixas, nor did it end then. Since our retirement in the fall of 1998, Ebba and I have been back to Crixas twice, once in 2003 and again in 2006, with opportunities to speak each time in the Presbyterian Church.

CHAPTER TWENTY-ONE

RETIREMENT TIME, A CRUCIAL YEAR IN OUR LIVES

*T*he year 1998 was a crucial year in our lives. Ebba and I were struggling with the decision: stay in Brazil or retire and return to the United States?

Our children were suggesting we retire, so their children could get to know their grandparents and we could get to know them. Ebba's health was a factor, too, perhaps she could fine help in the United States. She had not found a cause or cure in Brazil for the problems she had been experiencing for so long. These were valid reasons for retiring, but we were hesitant: there was still so much more we could accomplish in Brazil! But in the end, we decided to retire.

This meant selling or giving away everything we owned, except for selected items we wanted take to back with us. This process took several months since we had accumulated a lot of stuff over the years. Our piano was sold to the Second Baptist Church in the city of Anapolis. We held two or three garage sales to get rid of clothing and household items. The books we didn't send back to the United States were given to people, or sent to the libraries in the Institutes of Peniel and Macedonia. Most of our furniture was purchased by missionary colleagues. Daniel Schuring bought our car, a 1989 Monza.

In September of 1998, Lowell Denelsbeck took us to Goiania where, with very mixed emotions, we boarded a plane destined for the United States. Dan and Beatriz Steinman, our daughter and her husband, met us at the airport in Washington, DC.

At this time, we did not know where we would be living here in the USA. One possibility was in Englewood, Colorado where we had the home my parents lived in for over fifty years and in which I grew up from seven years of age until I went to Brazil. As it always had been wherever we moved, the house and property in Englewood needed considerable fixing-up before we could live in it. The drawback to living in Colorado was living so far from our children and grandchildren. This would defeat one of the main reasons we had retired.

We began looking at possibilities of settling in the Chesapeake, Virginia area, but could not find anything suitable. The Lord, however, was at work, orchestrating everything behind the scenes! We found a buyer for the house in Colorado, and that transaction made it possible for us to purchase a house in Chesapeake. Ebba and I ended up with a home that was beautiful and comfortable beyond our wildest dreams in an ideal location. We called it our 'Miracle Home' because of what God accomplished to make it a reality. We were now in driving distance to all our children.

Though we never regretted moving back home to our native land, Brazil remained close to our hearts, where for forty-seven years we worked in the fields *white unto harvest,* and where we were married and where our children were born. That's why we have been back to Brazil four times since we left in September of 1998.

The first time was in 2000; we stayed only nine weeks instead of the eleven we had planned. Our dear Brazilian friends, Senhor Eclidio and his wife, Adelina, loaned us a car to use while we were there. That was a great blessing! Our first stop, after leaving Anapolis, was the *Instituto Missionário Shekinah* in Mato Grosso do Sul where we spent several days. The next was Nonoai, where we had lived for many years. While there, Ebba became very ill. We were in the home of a missionary family who was working with the Kaingang near Nonoai when she took sick—so sick, Ebba thought she might die. We cut our trip short and returned to the States.

At this point, we still had not discovered the cause of the chronic dysentery she had suffered for almost twenty years. We made an appointment with a specialist in Chesapeake. After examining her, and doing a variety of tests, he concluded that Ebba had *celiac disease*, which meant she was suffering from gluten intolerance and must avoid wheat, barley, and rye products. There is no medication for this problem, but by following the proper dietary procedures, Ebba got along quite well once we found out what was going on.

Our next trip to Brazil began on October 25, 2002, and lasted eight months. We lived and worked at the *Instituto Biblico Peniel*, and assisted the personnel there any way we could, and enjoyed this ministry very much, which involved teaching and counseling among other things. We lived in a little house, located on the edge of the busy main street of the Institute. Our house was constantly full of students and staff!

Before settling in Peniel for that semester, we spent almost a month in Pernambuco with Ed and Maggie Harper, visiting former students of ours. We visited a couple involved in evangelism and church planting in the city of Paulo Afonso, in the state of Bahia, and another couple working with the Pancararu tribe not far from the city of Paulo Afonso. I had the opportunity to preach many times, even on the local radio station in the town of Águas Belas. Ebba broke a tooth a couple of days after we arrived in Águas Belas, and a dentist there did a crown for the tooth, and completed this job before we left: and we saw the hand of the Lord at the timing of it all.

We also spent a week at the Macedonia Bible Institute, and while there, I spoke in chapel services, and sat in on some of the classes. I was pleased to see how well the Brazilian teachers were doing. Early each morning, while it was still cool, Ebba and I took walks of forty-five minutes to an hour, reminiscing about the early days and laughing about the bats and termites we'd had to fight, and how beautiful everything was now.

In November, we flew to Brasilia where we were met by Lourival Abreu, better known by the name Batista, who took us to Anapolis. In Anapolis we stayed with Senhor Ecildio and his wife, Dona Adelina, for the rest of the month. Then, in December, we took a bus to Crixas.

We stayed with Dona Sebastiana and Senhor Antonio again, who had put us up on our last trip to Crixas. We had many visitors while we were there, and were invited to preach in the church. The visit to Crixas was brief, but delightfully busy!

A few days after we returned to Anapolis, we packed our things in the car that Senhor Ecildio had loaned to us, and took off for Nonoai. As in Crixas, our time in Nonoai was short, but full of opportunities: speaking in churches and holding meetings every place we went.

It was after these trips that we headed to Anapolis to return the car, loaned to us by Senhor Ecildio, and boarded a bus to Peniel, after purchasing a few things we would need while at the Institute. Arriving, we resumed the jobs of teaching and counseling for one semester.

The third trip to Brazil, we were there from January 2005 until July 2006, serving, once again, at the Peniel Bible Institute. We lived in the same little house, which had been upgraded. A beautiful, new tile floor was installed in the living room and new kitchen cupboards made the kitchen shine! We both taught classes, counseled, hosted students in our home, and again, helped in every way we could. The staff asked us to be pastors for the staff, and we found this not only enjoyable for us, but a blessing to the staff, as we talked and prayed with each one concerning their individual needs. Ebba was constantly asked to speak in ladies' meetings, leading prayer meetings and Bible studies.

While Cora Taylor was on furlough in the United States, she loaned us her car, and after she returned, the staff members who had cars, loaned them to us for trips to town for groceries or for doctor or dental appointments: those kinds of things. Besides my daily teaching responsibilities, I had many opportunities to preach at the Institute, as well as in several churches in the area.

We were able to visit Crixas again, and made one hurried trip to Nonoai, in the month of July with our daughter in law, Priscila, and two grandsons. Priscila and the two boys wanted to see where their father, Derly, had grown up and gone to school as a boy.

It was wintertime, and in southern Brazil that means, it gets cold! The car we rented for the trip did not have a heater, and we nearly froze to death on the way to Nonoai, but after a couple of days, the weather changed, and it began to warm up. On the way to Nonoai we stayed one night with Aldo and Lourdes Diligente, who live in the city of Guarapuava, in the state of Parana. Dona Lourdes had been Arlene and Beatriz's teacher in grade school in Nonoai many years before.

We returned to Peniel after that trip, and while there, Dalva, the girl we raised who was like a daughter to us, came to spend a week with us before we returned to the United States.

On all our short-term ministries in Peniel after retirement, one thing we found very rewarding, was to have students whose parents had been students of ours in the 1970's!

Our fourth trip to Brazil began in early July 2008 and ended May of 2009. We took a day flight this time from Miami to São Paulo, which proved to be much easier for Ebba. Marcos Tadeu Torres, a former student and colleague, met us at the airport and took us to his home that first night. The next day, he took us and our luggage to Peniel. The Institute gave us the same little house we had been given to live in on our previous visits. A new ceiling had been installed in the kitchen and hallway by this time. Though the house was small and did not have much counter space in the kitchen, Ebba made do, and was always inviting students and staff for delicious meals and snacks. Saturdays, she would prepare a large pan of lasagna, and there would be six or more students around our table to enjoy it. We always ate on the back porch because there was not room enough inside for larger groups.

We had gone to Peniel with the idea of staying one semester, but the staff asked us to stay for a second semester, and we did. This time, we stayed a total of ten months and we felt like it was one of the best and most profitable times we'd had on our visits to Brazil.

One highlight during this visit, was the weekend we spent in the city of Araras, São Paulo. I had the privilege of officiating at the twenty-fifth wedding anniversary of Pastor Elizeu Cantelmo, and his wife, Josete, former students from Peniel. This Anniversary Ceremony was on Saturday, and the next day I preached in Pastor Cantelmo's church. Missions was the topic of my sermon.

A couple of days before we left Peniel to return home, José Marcos Braga, the President of the Institute, said, "Alton, come back and stay longer!" Those words are still ringing in my ears.

One highlight of our last visit to Brazil was when Daniel and Beatriz Steinman, our daughter and her husband, joined us and stayed nine days with us at the Peniel Institute. Dan is the pastor of the Freedom Baptist Church of Chesapeake, Virginia. The church sent them on a mission trip to Brazil.

They spent almost a week in the Gavião tribal village in the State of Maranhão with Bill and Jean Wiederhoeft, who are supported by Freedom Baptist Church. The two couples went by car to Anapolis, enjoying their time together. Dan and Beatriz took a plane to São Paulo, and then went by bus to Peniel.

Dan preached in two churches in Jacutinga, as well as in Peniel, and I interpreted for him. Beatriz and Dalva had not seen each other for thirty years, so once again, Dalva came to Peniel from Santa Catarina. We had a wonderful time together the week Dalva was there.

On the afternoon of May fourth, 2009, Dan Templeton graciously took us in his big station wagon to the airport in São Paulo where Dan and Beatriz and Ebba and I boarded a United Airlines flight to Washington, DC. Early on May 5th, we were greeted by Al and Gayle Carver, who were awaiting our arrival, to take us back to Chesapeake!

When you add the total time of the four ministry trips back to Brazil after retirement to the forty-seven prior years, Ebba and I have spent just over fifty years in Brazil. I wish I could do it again. Glory to God for the privilege of serving Him!

Will I return to Brazil again? Only God knows, but while Ebba was still with me, before God took her home, we were praying about when to return.

Dear reader, I know this history is incomplete, and does not begin to tell all that transpired during the fifty years we worked in Brazil. I have tried, however, to include something from every phase or aspect of activity. My prayer is that you will be blessed, as I am, when I realize how much was accomplished, and still being accomplished among the tribal groups in Brazil. Also that you might be challenged and become involved, in some way, in this fascinating activity we call missions.

Written with a grateful heart by Alton Cothron